Springer Books on Professiona. ~~~~~~~

Edited by Henry Ledgard

Springer Books on Professional Computing

AT&T

Taming the Tiger

Software Engineering and Software Economics

Leon S. Levy

AT&T Bell Laboratories

Springer-Verlag
New York Berlin Heidelberg
London Paris Tokyo

Leon S. Levy
AT&T Bell Laboratories
Warren, NJ 07060

Series Editor
Henry Ledgard
Human Factors Ltd.
Leverett, Massachusetts 01054
U.S.A.

With 9 Figures

Printed and bound by R.R. Donnelley & Sons, Harrisonburg, Virginia
Printed in the United States of America.

9 8 7 6 5 4 3 2 1

ISBN 0-378-96468-1 Springer-Verlag New York Berlin Heidelberg
ISBN 3-540-96468-1 Springer-Verlag Berlin Heidelberg New York

Acknowledgment

As usual in any scientific endeavor, many people and institutions contribute directly and indirectly to any research effort. Some have a larger share which should be noted:

- Professor J.R. Clark of Fairleigh Dickinson University who introduced me to the discipline of economics and its modes of thought and who read early versions of this work and helped to improve it;

- Professor Todd Idson under whose guidance the chapter on transfer pricing was written;

- *AT&T Bell Laboratories* where I developed the notion of *ultra high programmer productivity techniques* and who encouraged this work by citing it in the distinguished staff award presented to me in 1983;

- *Ben Gurion University of the Negev* in Beer Sheba, Israel, where I was a visiting Professor in the academic year 1983–84 and where the first draft of this paper was composed, and particularly Professor Michael Lin who first furnished me with the proof of my generalized synergy theorem;

- *Fairleigh Dickinson University* where my studies in the M.B.A. program have contributed to my understanding of the managerial and economic aspects of software engineering;

- Dr. Martin Freeman of Signetics Corporation and Mike Bianchi of AT&T Information Systems who discussed many of these ideas with the author while they were in the formative stages;

Acknowledgment

- Dr. James B. Salisbury, of AT&T Bell Laboratories, who gave me moral support;

- my brother, Joel, who read portions of the manuscript and offered valuable comments; and, especially,

- my wife, Millie, without whose patience and encouragement none of this would have been possible.

Contents

Contents

Chapter 1

Introduction

A small program is presented to motivate the concerns for programmer productivity and program quality that are the central issues of this set of essays. The example is one which demonstrates the *performance* aspect of programming.

In order to achieve program quality, where a program is understood and known to be correct, we need a *primary program description*. This primary program description not only describes the program but is also used to generate the program. The method of applying primary program descriptions to produce programs is called *metaprogramming* and is described in Chapter 3.

In the later chapters, we show how the method can be analyzed from an economic point of view to address the issues of productivity as well.

1

Introduction

In thinking about programming over the last decade, I have concluded that very little is *known* about the process of programming or the engineering of software [1]. The consequence of having very little established truth to use as a basis for thinking about programming is that almost every conclusion must be reasoned out from first principles. Also, you cannot rely solely on textbooks but must use experimentation and direct observation to gain some experience with which to proceed.

It is also likely that if you proceed to examine the reality, you will conclude, as I and others have, that much of the accepted practice in the field is grossly inefficient. Moreover, in many cases, the quality is not very high, neither in the products nor in the documentation.

In the next few pages I talk through the development and modification of a very small program, less than one page at double spacing. The design and analysis that I discuss is a model of the development of larger programs. This process is very labor intensive and, consequently, the productivity must of necessity be low and the quality difficult to control.

---

[1] Much of the material in this introduction is taken from [Broome].

Introduction

The programs that most interest me are several orders of magnitude larger than the example program. If we are to find a way to radically improve both the quality and productivity of programming, then we must find a way to make programming less labor intensive. However, before considering solutions let us examine this small program fragment:

Example. The following "toy" program should serve to illustrate much of what is wrong with the current software practice. If I were to choose a larger program to make the point we would be overwhelmed by its sheer size. Here we can concentrate on some fundamentals.

The program is one which inverts a permutation [2]. It is

---

[2] A permutation is a rule which "rearranges" a set of numbers. The rule which takes 1 to 2, 2 to 3, and 3 to 1, is a permutation of the set of numbers 1,2, and 3. The inverse of this permutation is the rule which determines what number is permuted into the given number. The inverse permutation takes 1 to 3, 2 to 1, and 3 to 2. The way that the inverse permutation may be easily calculated is to arrange the permutation as follows:

1	2
2	3
3	1

To determine what the permutation is we can look for a number in the left hand column and find the number that it is permuted to by moving across the row into the right hand column. To determine the inverse problem, look in the right hand column to find the number and then move across the row into the left hand column.

convenient to represent such a permutation of numbers as an array, A, where `A[i]` stores the number to which `i` is permuted. In practice, if the set of elements being permuted is not too large one can construct the inverse permutation as a second array, B, and then write a simple program which proceeds through the array A and for each index `i` in A makes the assignment `B[A[i]] := i`. Thus, `B[A[1]] := 1`, or `B[2] := 1`. This method uses two memory cells for each element of the permutation, one cell for the original permutation, and one cell for the inverse element.

If the set of elements being permuted is large and you are interested primarily in computing the inverse permutation, then you may write a subroutine to invert the permutation, *in place*. While this subroutine is running, the values stored in the elements of A will be unpredictable, but when the subroutine has concluded, the element `A[i]` will contain the inverse of `i` under the permutation. The in place permutation inversion will use only one cell for each element. (Of course, after the inverse permutation has been computed the original permutation will not be available.)

Readers interested in more information about permutations, can see [Levy 1980c].

Introduction

Here is the body of a subroutine to invert a permutation:

```
1    for m := n step -1 until 1 do
2    begin
3            i := A[m];
4            if i < 0 then A[m] := -i
5            else if i <> m then
6            begin
7              k := m;
8              while i <> m do
9              begin
10                      j := A[i]; A[i] := -k;
11                      k := i; i := j;
12               end;
13               A[m] := k;
14        end
15   end
```

Program 1. Invert A Permutation in Place

Now each permutation consists of one or more disjoint cycles. An example of a permutation, A, with its cycle structure is shown in Figure 1.1.a. The corresponding inverse permutation, B, with its cycle structure is shown in Figure 1.1.b. The cycle structure of B is

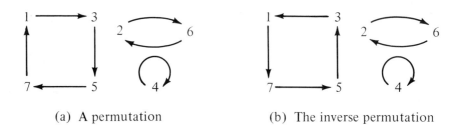

(a) A permutation   (b) The inverse permutation

Figure 1.1 A Permutation and its Inverse

similar to **A** except that the arrows are reversed.

Introduction

The algorithm of our initial in-place permutation inverter can be described as follows:

```
for each m between 1 and n do

        if the cycle beginning at m
                has not been inverted then
        invert and mark
                each element of the cycle (except for m)

        else remove the marker from this element.
```

This algorithm inverts one cycle at a time, marking each element with a negative sign (-). When the algorithm later encounters an element with a marker, the marker is removed.

Program 1 has few variables. The idea of the algorithm is simple but the program causes us difficulty. How do we know that the program is correct? How can we retain the link between the algorithm and the program so that when the program is written the design is not thrown away?

The communication medium between the programmer and the computer is often the source of the problem. When we must contort our ideas to fit the syntax of a particular programming language, the idea is sometimes lost. Luckily we are beginning to realize that a program's purpose is not to instruct the computer but to have the computer execute our program.

Nonetheless, even if we accept the constraints that machines and programming languages impose on us, something can still be done to better represent the idea of Program 1.

One major cause of errors in a program is the concern for (machine) efficiency. Only if we know that a program is correct can we then be concerned about efficiency. If a program is not correct, it matters little how fast it runs.

In line 5 of Program 1 there is a test for `i <> m` so that we can avoid inverting a singleton cycle. But the average number of singleton cycles in a permutation of size n is just 1, [Knuth]. So this attempt to increase efficiency has actually decreased efficiency!

Because of the early introduction of the variable, `i`, it is not readily apparent that the test `i <> m` is a test for a singleton cycle. An attempt such as this to avoid reevaluation of `A[m]` is usually unnecessary because most compilers can recognize a duplicate expression and avoid a recalculation for us.

In order to obtain a better program we should return to the design stage. Another outline of the algorithm is:

8

```
for m := 1 to n do
      if cycle at m has not been inverted  then
          invert and mark every element of the cycle
      remove the marker from this element
```

It is more natural to take m from 1 to n than to go the opposite way. We can avoid special cases by marking (with a minus sign (-)) *every* element of the cycle, whereas Program 1 leaves element m unmarked.

The most difficult part of Program 1 is that for chasing around a cycle, especially the part for moving from one element to the next. All ways of moving around a cycle are similar in that they have the following outline:

```
start at m
while not done do
begin
      process the current element
      move to the next element
end
```

As an example, consider the problem of finding an element x which we know to be somewhere in the cycle. The program part:

```
i := m;
while A[i] <> x do
    i := A[i];
```

will return i such that A[i] = x. Other than the array, A, and the value, x, this program part requires one other variable, the variable i. As we shall see, the number of additional variables increases with the complexity of the process.

As a second example of loop chasing, assume that we want to break a cycle into all singleton cycles. The program part

```
i := m;
j := A[i];
while A[i] <> i do
begin
    A[i] := i;
    i := j;
    j := A[i];
end
```

requires two additional variables, i and j. Before we modify $A[i]$ to be i we must have a way of getting to the next element, hence the need for previously saving this next element in j.

The program part for finding an element x does not modify the cycle so there is no statement comparable to $A[i] := i$ as in the last example; yet, both examples have a similar pattern of movement.

In both examples the conditions for loop termination accurately represent the functions of the program parts. In the first program part we desire to have $A[i] = x$. When this happens we leave the loop. In the second program part we must have $A[i] = i$. When this happens we leave the loop because this element (i) was previously visited.

When inverting a cycle we must have knowledge of three (adjacent) elements, so we need three additional variables: the current element, the last element (where we want the current one to point), and the next element (where the current one now points). The program part

```
i := m;
j := A[i];
k := A[j];
while A[j] <> -1 do
begin
      A[j] := -1;
      i := j;
      j := k;
      k := A[j]
    end
```

inverts a cycle and negates each element to indicate the visit. Note that the terminating condition (A[j] = -1) and the first statement of the loop (A[j] := -1;) are very similar.

The part of the loop body for moving to the next element is reminiscent of a centipede crawling. Note the effect of the loop body on a segment of a cycle, as shown in Figure 1.2.

We finally arrive at the program shown as Program 2, shown on pages 13-14.

begin

A[j] : = −i

i : = j

y : = n

K : = A[j]

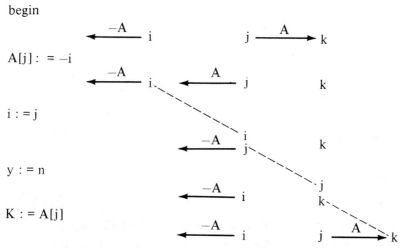

Figure 1.2 Graphic Representation of Cycle Inversion

```
1    for m := 1 to n do
2    begin
3        if A[m] > 0 then
4        begin
5            i := m;
6            j := A[i];
7            k := A[j];
8            while A[j] <> -1 do
9            begin
10               A[j] := -1;
11               i := j;
12               j := k;
```

```
13                    k := A[j];
14               end
15          end;
16          A[m]  := A[-m]
17     end.
```

Program 2: Invert a Permutation, A, in Place.

This program examines each element **m**. If the element at **m** is positive, then we have found a loop that has not been inverted and we invert it. Therefore, at line 16, **A[m]** will always be negative.

The assignment statements at lines 5-7 and at lines 11-13 point out that **i**, **j**, and **k** are adjacent elements of the cycle (the last, current, and next elements). The test on line 8, (**A[j] <> -i**), points out that the value **A[j]** is not what we wish it to be. The situation is thus remedied on line 11.

Not only is Program 2 easier to understand than Program 1, but it also executes faster. The execution time of Program 2 can be improved even more (by inverting **A[m]** outside the *while* loop), but it will then be a larger (more difficult to understand) program.

Primary Program Descriptions - The example of inverting a permutation shows that even relatively simple programs are difficult to understand and, consequently, will be very hard to certify with

Introduction

any degree of assurance. Wherein do the difficulties arise?

Undecidability of Equivalence

Given two programs, or a program and a specification, it is known that there is no algorithm - and hence no possibility of a program - to determine whether the program and its specification are equivalent. The consequence of this theoretical result is that we should find it difficult to compare a program and its specification, or to show that two programs are equivalent. For each of the programs given in the example, a proof that the program meets its specification is indeed somewhat difficult.

The Competence-Performance Dilemma

Another reason that it is hard to write correct programs is that we are often tempted to write programs that are about as complicated as we can handle. Precisely because these programs are at the limits of human performance, they are difficult to debug. Of course, the syntax of programming languages only deals with the competence aspect of language and ignores this "human engineering" dimension. Restricting program text to a single page, or eliminating *goto*'s can be only partial solutions.

15

Introduction

What You See Is Not What You Get

The program text presented as the solution to a problem does not indicate its derivation, or the underlying principles used to arrive at the program. This program *deep structure* [Levy 1977] is essential to an understanding of the program, and the correction of bugs almost invariably requires such an understanding. As noted in [Levy 1977], a program developed rationally at the level of deep structure and then optimized via transformations is perfectly acceptable, providing that the deep structure and transformations are part of the documentation.

It is particularly hard to develop and understand programs in systems that require the programmer to do optimizing transformations. An example which is generally familiar, is the one-pass vs. the two-pass assembler. The two-pass assembler is much clearer than the one-pass assembler, since the one-pass assembler is essentially a transformed and optimized version of the two-pass assembler.

Primary Program Descriptions

If this analysis is correct, then a proper methodology of program development to ensure correctness must be based on the following principles:

Introduction

i. There must be a document completely describing the program.

ii. The program description must be understood by its intended audience at a level well within the limits of the audience's performance.

iii. The documentation must include all of the deep structural information and all of the relevant transformations.

A description satisfying these criteria is a *primary program description* (PPD). No particular form is prescribed for the PPD as the following examples illustrate:

a. A payroll program may use an annotated decision table as a PPD.

b. A lexical scanner may use an annotated finite state transducer as a PPD.

c. A depth-first search algorithm may use an annotated pidgin-Algol program as a PPD.

d. Various flowcharts or structured flowcharts with appropriate commentary can serve as PPD's [Carberry].

The important point is that if different forms of PPD are used with the same program, then the correspondence between the PPD's must be established algorithmically. Moreover, there will generally be a syntax directed translation between

17

Introduction

PPD's using algebraic methods as described in Levy, [2].

These primary program descriptions form the desired specification components in the method of metaprogramming, discussed in Chapter 3.

Chapter 2

Unifying Themes

The two principal themes of this set of essays are:

- the need for a fundamental reassessment of software engineering based on emerging software technologies and a more fundamental understanding of the programming process;

- an economic analysis of the software development process that will provide criteria for selecting the best ways of achieving program quality and high productivity.

Myth - A belief or a subject of belief whose truths are accepted uncritically

Two themes pervade this series of essays. The first theme concerns software engineering and the nature of programming. Software engineering has been with us for about twenty years, long enough to have been tested in the industry. During those two decades much has happened in the technological fields related to software engineering, but the software crisis which software engineering was intended to resolve has not faded or diminished. It is time to reexamine the assumptions of software engineering and to search for new methods which will work.

The second theme is economics. Software economics has often been misconceived as the means of estimating the cost of programming projects. But economics is primarily a science of *choice*, and software economics should provide methods and models for analyzing the choices that software projects must make. If, as I believe, the technology of software is at the beginning of some major changes, then the software pricing models based on the experience of the past decade will become largely irrelevant, and the economics of choice will play a central role in software engineering.

2.1 Software Engineering

One regularly hears comparisons between the progress of hardware and the progress of software. Computer hardware has regularly shown improvements in the performance obtained for a given price at an accelerating rate. The microcomputers of today exceed the giant computers of the 1950's and 1960's in everything but price which has been reduced by between two and three orders of magnitude. And there is every indication that the next two decades will bring even more exciting developments.

The design and fabrication of computers have evolved so fast that a computer that is five years old is obsolete. It may still serve a useful function but if one goes out to buy a new computer, a five year old model will simply not do. And the new computers are built by highly automated plants, with the quality well-controlled, so that the maintenance headaches of the early hardware years are almost forgotten.

Contrast this progress in hardware with what we know of software. Software is still primarily a cottage industry, produced by hordes of programmers turning out hand-crafted code in much the same way that it was written at the time the term software engineering was coined [1]. The programming languages in which

---

[1] Popular folklore associates the term with the 1967 Nato Conference on Software Engineering.

most software is written were developed in the 1960's or early 1970's with, at most, minor revisions. And the data on software maintenance expenditures can only be called *horrifying*; figures range from a low of 50 % to as high as 80-90 %.

How can one explain that progress in hardware has been so fast, while progress in software has been painfully slow? In fact, this slow pace has led observers to predict a similar snail's pace to the end of the century. For example, [Ershov] says, "Given the existing productivity growth tendency and large underutilized reserves, doubling the programmer's productivity by the early 1990's and tripling it by the year 2000 seems realistic."

More important, what can we learn from the failure of software engineering to solve the problems that it has been addressing? How can we avoid a repetition of the past two decades of stagnation in software engineering? What are the *myths* about programming and software engineering that have impeded progress?

Perhaps the most prevalent misconception is contained in the notion of *continuity,* that programming over the next few decades will not change drastically. Clearly this can become a self-fulfilling prophecy, for if we continue to develop software as in the past then we probably will not make any significant progress on either software productivity or on software quality. Here, I see the automatic generation of program *fragments* as the most hopeful technique. This concept is developed more fully in the chapter on Metaprogramming. The metaphor for software production is a large assembly line with automated production of specialized components and the development of *transfer machinery* to assemble these components into complete packages. Only with this kind of automation can the labor-intensive nature of software be altered.

The second pervasive myth of software engineering is the model of the software development cycle contained in the so-called *waterfall model*. In the waterfall model, software development is decomposed into a series of phases starting with a requirements definition phase, followed by a specification phase, followed by a design phase, and only at this point, after considerable resources have been expended, are any programs actually written. The waterfall model is not *a priori* a deficient way of representing the development of software. But, in practice, it has turned out to be so, especially when innovative systems are being constructed. The requirements and specifications produce large quantities of documents that are often not read because of their volume and are difficult, if not impossible, to maintain. The waterfall model is examined in Chapter 5.

A more fundamental problem is the lack of understanding of the programming process. In the chapter on the Cartesian programmer and the hacker, I discuss this problem. It is a hopeful sign that in the past fifteen years, a variety of programming metaphors have emerged: functional programming, logic programming, object-oriented programming, and spreadsheets. More research is needed on how we solve problems in order to understand the role of programming languages and their relation to different modes of thinking. The myth of a common language for programming is that it is possible to find a single language or notation to program in. The experience of human problem-solving in many disciplines belies this notion. The variety of styles and notations in mathematics, for example, allows the solution of more problems than a single language or notation could.

While I have emphasized what I see as the myths of software engineering, I also see many hopeful signs. There is a growing awareness that software engineering has not accomplished what it set out to do. Increasingly, there is criticism of the waterfall model. And more systems are emerging that allow a combination of programming languages and styles to be combined in forming a software system.

In Chapter 4, I discuss the programming process and the need to accommodate diversity in programming styles. In Chapter 5, I present an overview of software engineering.

One important area in which I do not see any progress is in the productivity or quality of the documentation. Documentation is a significant part of software, but I see no hopeful signs. In the final chapter, I indicate what an approach to the documentation problem must be, but it will require much research to achieve significant results in this area.

2.2 Software Economics

Chapters 7-9 deal with economic issues. Economics provides some of the conceptual tools for analyzing the choices that software engineers face. In any software project, there is always a balance between short term and long term concerns. I believe that economic methods can help us to make enlightened choices.

Consider the waterfall approach to software development. It evolved as a development method to allow orderly management of the software cycle. The problem that it addressed was the premature coding of programs that would have to be changed as the full requirements of the system became clear. In other words, the short term gains of having some early code would be negated by the long term costs that that code would entail because it was not solving the right problem. The waterfall method attempted to solve this problem by applying some resources initially so that when the programs were actually written the time and effort invested would not be wasted.

However, what has happened is precisely the opposite of what was intended [2]. The software that was developed to the requirements and specifications may have met those specifications but did not satisfy the needs of the real users, either because the process of creating requirements and specification is inherently difficult or because the process took so long that the needs changed. The process of creating requirements and specifications tended to isolate the programmers from the actual needs of the users. If code were written early in the development cycle, that code might turn out to need extensive revision, but in the process of adapting it the real needs of the users would be identified because the users would be involved.

An economic analysis of the waterfall model might have identified its shortcomings. But that is a moot point now since there is a growing consensus that it is not the way to develop software. Rapid prototyping has solved the problem of premature investment in programming by reducing the costs of producing the early programs. However, if rapid prototyping is only a prelude to the use of a waterfall cycle, then the investment in developing the system following the prototype phase may be largely wasted as the users'

---

[2] This is an example of what economists term *secondary effects*.
 Secondary effects: Economic consequences of an initial economic change, even though they are not immediately identifiable. The impact of secondary effects will be felt only with the passage of time. [Gwartney], p. 9.

needs change. Rapid prototyping can only succeed if it is followed by rapid fabrication of the software, a process that must require larger investment in the tools for building and assembling the software system.

The method of metaprogramming is presented in Chapter 3 as a response to the problems induced by the waterfall method of developing software. In brief, the method of metaprogramming builds a disciplined development method on the basis of the models that are defined in the rapid prototyping phase of a project. The management of this programming process relies on the tools of managerial economics to make decisions of resource allocation and planning.

Chapters 7-8 are an economic analysis of the method of *metaprogramming*, showing how it can use the methods of rapid prototyping and rapid fabrication to produce systems that are both economical and of high quality. Metaprogramming is a direct attack on the labor intensive method of producing software. In many cases it is more economical to write programs to create applications than it is to create the applications directly, and applications generated by program generators have fewer bugs. Moreover, if the machinery is created to produce the application and the requirements change, the system can be regenerated using the same program generators.

2.3 Quasi-Expert Systems

There is a large class of programming systems that are particularly interesting. These programs lie in the general field of *artificial intelligence* and, more particularly, in the subfield of that discipline known as *cognitive science*. These *expert systems* have been the subject of considerable interest recently, both because of the appearance of some such systems that have been commercially or scientifically successful and because the plans for the fifth generation Japanese computers [3] are directed to the construction of computers for expert systems.

2.3.1 Expert Systems

2.3.1.1 What Is an Expert System [4]? A definition of an expert system as given by [Banner] is:

> An expert system is a computing system which embodies organized knowledge concerning some specific area of human expertise, sufficient to perform as a skillful and cost-effective

---

[3] See, e.g., [ACM], for a series of articles on the Japanese fifth generation computer project.

[4] [Kinnucan] presents a nontechnical introduction to the subject of expert systems and knowledge-based engineering.

consultant.

Typical features of expert systems include the following:

- knowledge embodied in units that are meaningful to experts, including heuristics [5].

- knowledge separate from "inference engine";

---

[5] *Heuristic* or "ars inveniendi" was the name of a certain branch of study, not very clearly circumscribed, belonging to logic or to philosophy, often outlined, seldom presented in detail, and as good as forgotten today. The aim of heuristic is to study the methods and rules of discovery and invention. A few traces of such study may be found in the commentators of Euclid; a passage of *PAPPUS* is particularly interesting in this respect. The most famous attempts to build up a system of heuristic are due to *DESCARTES* and to *LEIBNIZ*, both great mathematicians and philosophers. Bernard *BOLZANO* presented a notable detailed account of heuristic. The present booklet is an attempt to revive heuristic in a modern and modest form.

Heuristic, as an adjective, means "serving to discover."   - Polya, *How to Solve It*, p. 112

Heuristic rules are plausible rules for solving problems which are not necessarily guaranteed to work. For example, a heuristic rule for getting from A to B is to find the shortest path on the map that leads from A to B and follow that route. This rule often succeeds, but fails under adverse road conditions, detours, accidents, etc.

- ability to reason with uncertainty;

- ability to explain itself;

- user-friendly, accessible to experts without computer proficiency;

- having natural language interface.

2.3.1.2 Typical Expert Systems The class of systems known as expert systems comprises programs whose information content and problem-solving ability approximates that of a specialist, albeit within a suitably limited domain. Some of the better known expert systems are:

Dendral   A system for analyzing organic chemical compounds from mass spectrography data.

Mycin   A medical diagnosis system that attempts to act as a consultant on internal medicine.

R1   A system that configures computing systems assuring proper space, power, accessibility, etc.

Prospector   A system that analyzes mineralogical data

2.3.2 Framework of an Expert System The organization of an expert system can be visualized as in Figure 2.1 [Gevarter]:

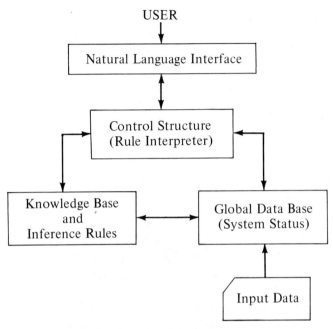

Figure 2.1. Organization of an Expert System

The basic design of the expert system requires a choice of *knowledge representation* that is usable by the machine and, at the same time, is understood by the expert. Some of the techniques that have been used are:

Production Systems   A set of rules of the form: CONDITION =>
                        ACTION.

31

Unifying Themes

Predicate Logic   A set of statements of logical relationships
                       stated in a formal syntax.

Frame Systems   A set of descriptions of the relationships that
                       exist.

  Since an expert system tries to isolate the body of knowledge
from its application, [6], means for applying the knowledge to
problems must be incorporated. Some of the methods chosen are:

Forward Chaining   Proceeding forward from the data to the
                       conclusions.

Backward Chaining   Attempting to support a conclusion, and
                       seeking confirming evidence.

Blackboard Model   Partitioning a problem, and working on parts
                       of the problem independently.

  After the framework of the expert system is set, the acquisition
of the knowledge that must be included can take from one to ten
years. This phase requires continual adjustment and modification of
the data and heuristics because:

---

[6] The number of rules in a typical expert system ranges from about 300 to
    800.

- the knowledge to be included changes with the state-of-the-art;

- the experts are not able to formulate the heuristics properly without trial-and-error;

- knowledge representation is often a difficult programming problem because of the unexpected interaction of rules.

2.3.2.1 Characteristics of Expert Systems The typical expert system is a large program which evolves over a period of years. Typically the construction of an expert system requires the interaction of computer scientists with experts in the domain of the application. Since the problem-solving techniques in the application domain are not formalized, considerable iteration is required to achieve a good level of performance.

Expert systems are generally intended to be used by non-experts for purposes of consultation. It is often assumed that the users are not especially 'computer literate' or do not care to become involved with the details of the program. Thus a significant portion of the expert system is a natural language interface.

Expert systems are intended to solve difficult problems in which considerable reasoning is involved. To be believed, the 'expert' must be able to explain the reasoning by which the conclusions were deduced. This introspective capability is also needed for the human experts who are trying to improve the system's accuracy. When the system reaches a conclusion that is at variance with the conclusion of the human experts, the assumptions and inference rules that led to that conclusion must be modified.

2.3.2.2 Relevance of Expert Systems to this Work Expert systems are selected as a particular class of software systems that merits study because:

1. They are currently leaving the research environment and entering the commercial world.

2. They are large systems, requiring a significant investment and promising a large return on that investment.

3. The technology of expert systems is evolving more rapidly than that of other software systems.

4. Within expert systems one sees most clearly the application of *data-driven* programming allowing the decomposition of a program into a fixed control structure and a variable data structure.

I hope that the approach discussed, particularly in Chapter 3, is assessed by its applicability in managing the development of expert systems. I shall say more about decompositions later, but it is clear that they are of fundamental importance in the development of large systems.

2.3.2.3 Quasi-Expert Systems There is also a large class of software systems which share the software engineering characteristics of expert systems. I call these systems *quasi-expert systems*. In a quasi-expert system the overall software architecture remains fixed while many of the logical transformations performed on the data change. Many large software systems can be classified as quasi-expert systems.

As one example of a quasi-expert system, consider a decision support system where the data base organization is fixed by the initial systems design but many of the algorithms are subject to change [Keen].

A more familiar example of a quasi-expert system is an operating system, where the hardware and kernel are fixed by the initial systems design but the rest of the system is adaptable to different configurations. A previous work [Freeman 1978] has described the decomposition of an operating system into a fixed, structural component and a variable set of *policies* and *actions*.

These systems are not expert systems because:

1. They may not be interactive.

2. The tasks they perform may not be 'expert tasks.'

3. There may be no natural language interface.

4. There may be no explanatory mode.

However, these systems have the following features in common with expert systems:

1. They contain a large number of rules and transformations.

2. The rules are often difficult to formalize and perhaps changeable.

3. Extensive 'tuning' of the system is required.

Chapter 3

Metaprogramming

Metaprogramming is the technique used to achieve the *primary program descriptions* described and motivated in Chapter 1. In metaprogramming a high-level description of a part of an application is described in some conceptual model and the programs to realize that model are produced by program generation techniques that have evolved in compiler technology.

The role of conceptual models is to isolate detail and allow the programming of an application to proceed concurrently with the definition of the details. First, the details are likely to change in many applications, and a system can be stable only if it is insensitive to those perturbations. Second, the details are of interest to users of the system, but not to many programmers. The model provides a language which is concise and precise for the communication between systems analysts and programmers.

There are several features of metaprogramming which are important. First, it seems unlikely that any single conceptual model can adequately capture the diverse aspects of a large application. Therefore, the assembly of a number of program components into one large program is an important technology which must be developed. Second, the rationale for metaprogramming is that it provides economies of scale in programming. While this is true for large parts of many applications, it is not necessarily true for all parts of all applications. So many applications, it is not necessarily true for all parts of all applications. So the economics of metaprogramming becomes an important part of the software engineering.

In this chapter, I present the metaprogramming method, summarize two projects that used the method, and present an economic analysis of the method.

Metaprogramming, defined as creating application programs by writing programs that produce programs, is presented as the basis of a method for reducing software costs and improving software quality [1]. The method starts with a rapid prototyping phase in which selected representative parts of the application are prototyped, followed by a 'tooling up' phase, during which the *metaprogramming* occurs. The final phase is the production of the application programs using the software tools and techniques of the *metaprogramming* phase.

We summarize the experience of two projects that support the assertion that *metaprogramming* is an efficient way to produce programs, since these projects used *metaprogramming* in their development. We also present the outlines of an economic theory which justifies this approach, and shows how to do a cost/benefit analysis of the method.

3.1 The Problem

Software costs are perceived as being exorbitant, and software quality is considered to be poor. The most important problem for software engineering is to find ways to significantly reduce the costs of software while at the same time significantly enhancing software quality by reducing its error rate [Boehm 1973], [Boehm 1981].

It is also generally accepted that the problems of software do not reside in the product *per se*. Each of the elements out of which the software is composed may be sound, while the software as a whole may be unsatisfactory. As [Fairley] has noted, "Software has no physical properties, it is not subject to the laws of gravity or the laws of electrodynamics." So, if the problem does not lie in the constituents of the software product, it must come from the process by which that product is produced [2].

Therefore, the problem with the software being produced is rooted in the process of creating the software. In order to solve the

---

[1] This chapter appeared originally in [Levy 1986].

[2] Another way to see that you cannot determine the quality of the software from an examination of the product is as follows:

   Suppose that we are given two programs, A and B, and we know that A is a quality product, perhaps because it was proven correct, but we are not sure about B, except that it is claimed that B is exactly equivalent to A. If the claim is true, then the behavior of program B will be identical to the behavior of program A, so that B is also presumably a quality product - at least by any reasonable operational standard. But it is well-know that there is no algorithmic procedure to decide whether in fact the programs A and B are, in general, equivalent.

software problem we must modify the process of software development: we need a better *method*. Indeed, one approach to improving software quality - with particular emphasis on correctness - attempts to emulate mathematical methods of proof, but, as has been noted in the literature, historically mathematical proofs have not been error-free [Lakatos] nor are they easy to formulate.

3.2 What Is a Method?

A software design method is [Wasserman]:

> A systematic procedure that [soware developers] can follow from the original concept of a system through its specification, design, development, operation, and evolution.

In more detail a design method is [Freeman 1976]:

- A structured decision making process that

- makes the design visible and

- is related to organizational procedures and

- makes the design objectives visible and

- keeps the process well-organized.

By providing a (management) discipline to help control the software development process, a method contributes to the

41

objectives of lower cost and better quality.

3.3 The Class of Programs Considered

While the general principles and objectives of a software development method may be the same for most projects, the specific embodiment of the method will probably vary with the characteristics of the specific product being developed. The class of programs considered here are those which model a complex, synthetic set of rules. (A set of rules would be complex if no notation is known that can concisely describe it, and it is synthetic if the rules are man-made.) Almost any administrative unit has a set of rules that can serve as an example; the set of rules for preparing income tax is a familiar one. In a program to compute income tax, the inputs would consist of the data that are used in preparing a tax return: all sources of taxable income and all the relevant deductions. The output of the program would be the complete (set of data required in the) tax form, or possibly a completed set of tax forms.

The set of rules of the JMOS application, described in [Levy 1985], are another good example. In the JMOS application, which calculates the work credit for construction jobs, the rules for calculating the time required and the value assigned to the work are determined by administrative guidelines depending on a complex combination of the factors involved in the construction work. Furthermore, advances in construction techniques or technology

42

require regular updating of the computational rules. The input to the job credit calculations of JMOS are the values of the set of factors determining the time and value for the particular construction task, such as material type and quantity, type of construction, physical environment, etc. The output of the program is a list of the work credits broken down into different categories.

In the software for such a system one must consider:

1. The initial description of the system being modeled is probably incomplete.

2. The description is wrong in some details.

3. Many items in the description will change during the life of the software.

The fact that, for the type of system being considered, it is impossible to write a complete, correct specification at the beginning of the software generation process is crucial to the choice of development method, because it means that the method must accommodate change in the software -- or the software must be rewritten [3].

The magnitude of the software considered is from 5,000 lines of code upwards, and the development involves a team of programmers for at least one year. This implies that the investment in the software is sufficient that it will be modified and adapted -- not rewritten -- over a period of at least five years, and much of the modification will be made by programmers who did not develop the original product.

3.4 Some Typical Cases

The two cases summarized below are projects in which the techniques of *metaprogramming* were used with significant productivity returns. The experience on these projects agrees with

---

[3] [Jackson] provides a critique of some of the better known functional design techniques. They are:

> 1. difficult to execute
> 2. not amenable to change
> 3. do not provide a clear distinction between design and implementation.

On the characteristic of changeability, see also [Parnas].

[Zave] also provides a thorough critique of the top-down software development method contrasting it with a method based on an *operational specification*. We discuss the relation between *metaprogramming* and operational specifications later.

claims of order-of-magnitude productivity gains for application generators that appear in the literature [Cardenas], [Rice], [Bassett]. For example, [Bassett] states that he achieved "production quality commercial software at rates exceeding 2,000 lines of debugged COBOL per day (including systems design time)."

Details of the programs of these two cases are contained in [Levy 1980] and [Levy 1985]. Here we are more interested in the general characteristics of the method.

3.4.1 CARL CARL, Computer Automated Route Layout, described in detail in [Levy 1980], is a medium-sized program (~45,000 lines of source code) written in 1979-80. The CARL program produces a representation of the loop plant of a telephone company in the form of computer-output microfilm. The initial version of the completed program written in RATFOR was developed by five programmers in approximately 30 programmer/months for an effective productivity rate of ~1,500 lines/person/month, including the time to produce the prototype.

3.4.2 JMOS JMOS, Job Management Operations System, is a large program (> 250,000 lines of source code). JMOS is an on-line operational support system to aid regional telephone company construction and engineering processes by tracking and managing construction work [Ehrenreich]. One module of this program, which analyzes data from engineering drawings and computes the work content of the construction job, is described in detail in [Levy 1985]. This module (~16,500 lines of *dense* PL/1 source code) [4] was developed by means of a code generator written for this project. The code generator translates an 850 page specification into PL/1 code [5].

The specification that the code generator uses as input is written in propositional logic. A typical condition in the specification is the following:

---

[4] Since the code is machine generated and the program is maintained by modifying the specification, the code generator does not format the code for readability and produces code with much less white space).

[5] A typical page of the specification contains 15-25 lines of logical conditions like those shown below, a header describing the work category, and material quantity, and about half a page of descriptive commentary. The descriptive commentary is ignored by the code generator, but is helpful to system engineers revising the specifications.

```
masktype = epw &
<like_cable> = 'true' &
{ plaatn = ctrb |
  plaatn = ctrm |
  plaatn = ctrh |
  plaatn = ctr |
      {  wrkenv = b &
      plaatn = stan &
      pacclass = c  &
      OPF(bu_cbl_plc_mth,arg1) ~= plow
  }
}
```

This notation was easily learned by non-programmers. In fact, all of the specifications of this form were written by people who were familiar with the application but were not programmers.

In fact, even this somewhat cryptic shorthand - see [Levy 1985] for clarification - was prepared with the assistance of a more abbreviated shorthand that was expanded by an editing script.

3.4.3 A Higher Level Description Both the CARL and the JMOS programs depended heavily on constructing a higher level description of the application and on writing a translator to produce the actual code. We call this technique *metaprogramming*, in which the programmer's effort is primarily in the development of application-code generators to produce the deliverable software. As we shall see, *metaprogramming* is an efficient way to produce software. It also produces high-quality, uniform programs because each program produced is a test of the translation process itself. Furthermore, change is controlled because a change in implementation is typically made in only one place - in the code generator - rather than in many places in the object programs.

3.5 The Method

The method embodied in the two examples given above may be summarized as follows:

Only the requirements needed to construct a prototype are fixed initially. The prototype has the architecture of the final system in terms of the database structure and top-level program control structure. This prototype is Brooks' throw away system [Brooks].

Once the prototype is completed and the form of the final system is fixed, a set of tools - program generators - are built. These program generators allow the real system to be built directly from specifications which serve as input to the generators. System modification is done by changing the input to the generators.

3.5.1 Deciding What Is Needed The initial phase of the method is analogous to a feasibility study. In this phase the form of the solution is determined - its architecture - and the components needed to implement that solution are identified. During this phase the abstract form of the program is determined. (For example, a communications protocol or a lexical analyzer may be modeled as finite-state machine.) If there is concurrency in the program, the forms of communication and synchronization are established. Also, the types of input/output and database routines are fixed.

In the CARL project, the initial phase established the use of Liskov's clusters [Liskov 1977] as the programming technique and defined a virtual memory hierarchy for the implementation. At this stage one could develop the data dictionary and specify the functions to be produced by the code generator during the next phase of the project.

In the JMOS project, the initial phase led to the concept of an inverted decision table as the primary specification form. (An inverted decision table is a top-down form of a decision table in which, for each possible output, the inputs needed to derive that output are listed. This contrasts with a standard, or bottom-up, decision table in which all possible input combinations are listed with the corresponding outputs.) This primary specification is the primary program description of Chapter 1.

The two examples suggest several conclusions:

1. The method is not restricted to a single style of programming or a single abstract model of computation.

2. The initial phase will include some exploratory programming, or *rapid prototyping*, to establish feasibility and explore alternative models.

3. The use of a *metaprogramming* method makes it necessary to choose computational models.

It is possible that that the prototype will lead to unwarranted conclusions that will force revision when all the needed details have been added. However, that is a risk which is associated with any decisions that are taken in any design method: they cannot be fully validated until the product is complete. The risks associated with *metaprogramming* do not appear to be greater than those of other development methods.

3.5.2 Tooling Up The tooling up phase begins once the form of the product has been determined and the software needed to produce it has been identified. If it has been determined during the initial phase that the abstract model of the software is a finite-state machine, then during the tooling up phase a set of programs that will produce the final code from a compact finite-state specification will be developed.

Once these tools have been developed and tested, it is possible to modify the details of the specification, as long as the modifications stay within the bounds of the model. For example, in the finite state machine model, the code generator may have a limit on the number of allowable states or inputs, and the specification will only be variable within those limits.

3.5.3 Production   The production phase should resemble an automated assembly line. Ideally, the set of tools developed during the tooling-up phase should now be able to start with a specification file and, using that specification as the input, produce and test the deliverable software product. In both the CARL and JMOS projects much of this objective was accomplished, but the assembly line was not fully automated. In the economic analysis, the decision not to fully automate the production of the software product is explained. Intuitively, the 20/80 rule seems to apply: it takes about 20% of the effort to automate the generation of 80% of the code, and that is the part that is worthwhile to do.

As is usually the case with most computational models, there are aspects of the application that are not described most efficiently within the computational model. Typically, for example, decision table processors have the ability to call subroutines coded in an algorithmic high-level language. The inverted decision table processor also has 'hooks' that allow hand-coded routines to be called from within the automatically generated code. In general, the decision as to what parts of the application should be generated automatically is an economic one (see below, the section on the economic justification) since the marginal returns from automation decrease as the percentage of automated code increases. This effect arises from the increasing difficulty of automating the last parts of the application.

The specification file should be readable by the people responsible for the functions of the software. (As noted above, some end users were comfortable with the propositional logic notation. For those who were not, a rather simple-minded program was written by the author to translate the propositional logic into an English-like form, but some post-processing would be needed to polish the language.) If the deliverable software can be generated and regression tested directly from the specifications, this will allow changes to the specification to be retrofitted to the software and will facilitate maintenance and upgrading of the product. In particular, it is highly desirable that there should be only one primary description of the function of the software and that it should be possible to guarantee that the software matches its specification.

3.6 Why Metaprogramming Works

There are several reasons why *metaprogramming* works:

1. It makes a program changeable within the limits of the code generator. New versions of a program can be expected to be as robust as the initial releases because no 'patches' are made to the code. It is always recompiled from the specifications.

2. It provides the programmer with leverage by increasing the ratio of the size of delivered program to the size of the primary program description. In both of the projects cited, the combined size of both the specification files and the code generation programs are about one tenth of the size of the delivered software.

3. It forces the programmer to think about the structure of the program and the process of software creation and thus focuses attention on productivity and quality.

4. Programming at the meta-level can better utilize the skills of trained computer scientists since the development of the code generators is similar to the construction of other program translators.

3.7 Limits of the Method

Ideally, the method should produce a software machine whose input is a high-level specification and whose output is an optimized, tested, and documented deliverable product. This objective is probably not realizable in the current state-of-the-art. Documentation is one of the limiting factors since a specification acceptable to a program is probably unacceptable to human readers and would require post-editing.

Metaprogramming depends on the choice of a suitable computational model for programming the application, the choice of an appropriate notation for expressing the computation, and the development of a code generator that can translate the notation into executable code. Applications generally can not be represented in a single computational model and notation because the expressive power of a notation is usually limited to a part of an application. For example, in both the CARL and JMOS applications there are complex network algorithms that are programmed directly in the algorithmic language and not in the *metaprogramming* language. A rough estimate is that 10-15% of an application that can be metaprogrammed will have to be handled in this way.

In practice, the method often falls short of even the attainable limit because, as noted above, complete automation of the software production process may not be the most economical solution. In the next section I discuss the economics of the *metaprogramming* method.

3.8 The Economic Justification [6]

There are a number of criteria which may be used to quantitatively evaluate a software method. The criterion that we choose here is to minimize the firm's software development costs over the ensemble of anticipated changes and enhancements during the lifetime of the program. The conjecture is that minimizing development costs over all anticipated changes and enhancements will reduce testing, maintenance, and other costs.

3.8.1 Marginal Cost = Marginal Revenue A basic principle of managerial economics is that one should continue in a given activity so long as the benefit to be derived from the last unit of activity exceeds the cost of that unit of activity [Truett], [Gwartney]. These incremental units are referred to as the marginal units. For example, a producer should continue to produce additional units of a given item so long as each additional item being produced is profitable; in other words, the marginal revenue produced from selling one additional unit exceeds the marginal cost of producing that additional unit. Using this principle, it is possible to determine the production quantity of an item by finding the production quantity where the marginal cost equals the marginal revenue.

We can directly apply the principle of equating marginal cost and marginal revenue to the problem of producing software as follows: During the tooling up phase we are incurring the costs of producing software tools that are not deliverable software products. By extending the tooling up phase we would be able to reduce the cost of the production phase in which the deliverable product itself is constructed, since we could produce tools that would further increase the productivity of programmers. How do we know when to stop the tooling up? We equate marginal cost and marginal revenue. So long as an additional month of software tool development is expected to give us a gain in productivity whose value exceeds the cost of that incremental development, we should spend that additional month of tool development.

3.8.1.1 Program Model Chapter 8 presents a model that allows the calculation of the optimum investment in the tooling up phase. The model calculates the productivity of a project as a function of

---

[6] The economic theory is developed in greater detail in Chapters 7-9.

the investment in software tools. Defining the productivity of a
single programmer as $P(t)$, we assume that $P(t + 1)$ is greater than
$P(t)$ with the dependence of the form

$$P(t+1) = f(n) * \{a + b*t + c*P(t)\} * P(0)$$

where a, b, and c are constants, t is time treated as discrete monthly
intervals, n is the number of programmers, and $f(n)$ is a
communication loss factor because it is generally agreed that as the
number of programmers on a project is increased, there is a
decreasing return to scale. In the model $f(n)$ is chosen to be $n/(1 +
k*log(n))$ since $f(n)/n$ should be monotonically decreasing; i. e. the
output per programmer decreases as the number of programmers is
increased. The equation for the productivity says that productivity
grows as a monotonic function of the programming effort invested to
increase productivity. (The constants to be used in the equation are
difficult to determine, as are all constants for calculating
programmer productivities, but the form of the equation allows
parametric studies of the effects of investment in productivity to be
made.)

A program based on that model allows one to study the effects of
investing in software productivity on a project. (The program also

accounts for the growth of staff during the project and the cost of development funds.) For example, using the program, for a project to produce a 50,000 line program starting with a staff of five programmers, the model [7] projects that the most efficient method of producing the software is to spend the first sixteen months in the tooling up phase and the next seven months in the production phase. This is calculated to be twice as efficient as developing the code directly, without a tooling up phase.

In fact, the model appears to be quite conservative, and actual gains realized on the projects cited and others mentioned in the literature are much larger. Indeed, the larger a project is the more that it has to gain from the up front investment.

3.8.1.2 Analytic Model Simplified analytic models of productivity can also be used to get a qualitative estimate of the effects of investing in software productivity. Suppose that a fixed amount of resources, n, is available to produce a program, C. Of these n resources, m may be used initially to enhance productivity, to increase productivity from $f(0)$ to $f(m)$. The product, C, is then

---

[7] The parameters used in this model were: a = b = 0, c = 0.05, k = 0.5, and an initial programming rate of 200 lines per staff-month. The comparison is with a COCOMO model of an embedded system.

given by

$$C = (n - m) * f(m)$$

so C is maximized by choosing

$$\frac{m}{n} = 1 - \frac{f(m)}{n * f'(m)}$$

This analytical model can be solved for simple cases like linear or exponential growth of productivity. If we assume that

$$f(m) = f(0) * e^{r * m}$$

then C is maximized by choosing

$$m = n - \frac{1}{r}$$

where r has the dimensions of staff/year and $1/r$ is the number of staff years to double productivity on the project divided by the natural logarithm of 2. So in the case of an exponential model almost all the time should be spent on productivity enhancement, except for the interval $1/r$ when the actual software product is generated.

3.8.2 On the Notion of Synergy [8] The claims of the efficiency of the *metaprogramming* method would seem, at first glance, to be extravagant. The cost of producing the programs becomes quite

---

[8] The concept of synergy presented here was first developed in [Levy 1982] and a more general formulation is presented in Chapter 7.

small once the tools are in place, and at that point claims of several orders of magnitude gain in programmer productivity can be found in the literature, as noted above. Indeed, if the gains are so substantial why has the method not prevailed universally?

To explain the apparent lack of impact of the enhanced productivity, consider the effect of an increase in programmer productivity on a large project. Suppose that the programming is 50% of the project effort. In that case, even an infinite increase in programmer productivity would have no more than the effect of doubling the overall productivity. The net result is that the less productive elements limit the overall productivity.

Now consider the following hypothetical scenario: Given a software project that consists of two equal components where each of the components separately proposes to double its productivity. A calculation of the effective gain of doubling the productivity of either component shows that the overall project gain due to the increases of productivity of that component is 4/3. (To see that this is so, compute the productivity as the ratio of the work to be done divided by the effort required. Then, in the comparison, the numerator does not change but doubling the productivity of one component changes the denominator to 3/4.) Even multiplying the two productivity gains appears to give an overall gain of 16/9. But, in fact, there is a synergistic effect that results in an overall gain of two when each components doubles its productivity, since it is clear that if each component doubles its productivity the overall productivity will be doubled.

The implication of the synergistic effect is to underestimate the productivity gains of production factors taken in isolation. The gain in productivity in a project cannot be calculated, as it often is, by multiplying the gains of the individual contributions. This may account for the fact that techniques like *metaprogramming* have not been as extensively used as they should be. Because of synergy, the joint contribution of a number of productivity gains exceeds the product of the gains taken separately. Furthermore, in considering a method it is particularly important to consider its impact on the least productive factors. In this case, the potential of the *metaprogramming* method to reduce test, maintenance, and documentation costs is a critical factor.

On the other hand, the synergy can be understood as what economists refer to as an *externality* [9]. An improvement in the rate of programming raises the value of subsequent improvements. So a possible additional value of *metaprogramming* is that it justifies added investment in the other software factors.

---

[9] [Samuelson] defines externality as "an activity that affects others for better or worse, without those others paying or being paid for the activity."

3.9 Comparison with the Operational Approach

[Zave] has described an operational specification as the basis for a software development method. The operational specification is a functional model of the application. After the operational specification is synthesized,, the role of the software development is to build a set of transformers which will construct the desired software product from the operational model with the same functions but within the constraints of the physical system on which the product is to be run.

Metaprogramming also sees the final software product as being generated from a higher level specification. But, in contrast to the operational method, it sees the form of the high level specification and the feasibility of constructing the transformers as the crucial elements whose existence must be demonstrated by prototyping a critical subset of the application. Furthermore, it is not necessary to build the entire system but only enough to validate the approach. However, the part of the system that is prototyped must be produced much as it will appear in the final product.

Recall that the applications for which we are considering *metaprogramming* for are characterized by incomplete, sometimes erroneous, and changeable specifications. It is desirable to have a concise representation of the application, whose details may change but whose structure does not. *Consequently, major emphasis in*

62

metaprogramming is on the choice of computational model.

3.10 Conclusion

We have presented a method of developing software by:

1. creating a rapid prototype

2. identifying the tools needed to generate a product

3. building those tools and enhancing programmer productivity

4. automatically producing the deliverable software product.

An economic rationale is presented in support of this method showing why it can produce higher quality software at lower cost.

Not yet discussed is how *metaprogramming* relates to the present managerial structure for software development in which the models are developed before the detailed project planning and scheduling can be undertaken. One would expect that, like other rapid prototyping methods, it will require the initial phase to be treated rather loosely, with more detailed planning and management controls once the feasibility phase has been passed.

Chapter 4

The Cartesian Programmer and the Hacker

The literature of programming contains a rich variety of approaches to programming. In this chapter I explain two fictitious but representative notions of programming as being rooted in deeper philosophic and psychological factors. I also consider briefly the consequences of such an analysis.

4.1 Introduction [1]

This chapter describes *programming* as seen from several different perspectives and interprets some of the literature on *software engineering* and *programming methodology* from these points of view. Here I have chosen to simplify the situation by discussing two extreme views of programming.

The dichotomy that I have drawn is between the 'rationalist' and 'empiricist' approaches to programming. But this dichotomy must be understood as a simplification of a much more complex reality, since there are more dimensions to personality types, and since people rarely are at one extreme or the other in any dichotomy. In the later sections of the chapter, some suggestions for accommodating both views of programming are discussed.

In Section 4.2 programming, as seen from the rationalist and empiricist points of view is presented. In Section 4.3 the different components of *semiotics* as seen from these perspectives are developed. In Section 4.4, multilingual systems are proposed as a means for encouraging these diverse approaches to programming.

_____

[1] An earlier version of this chapter was presented in [Levy 1980]

4.2 What is Programming?

4.2.1 The Rationalist View

Rationalism - a method, or very broadly, a theory of philosophy, in which the criterion of truth is not sensory but intellectual and deductive. Usually associated with an attempt to introduce mathematical methods into philosophy, as in Descartes, Leibniz, and Spinoza [Runes].

The rationalist programmer sees programming as a pure mental exercise. The role of the computer in this exercise is to establish the set of allowed options in the exercise. Whenever possible the computer structure used in the exercise should be simple and uniform.

Stated somewhat differently, the rationalist programmer starts with the conception of programming as an activity performed independently of the machine. In principle, one runs the program only as means of checking on the accuracy of one's mental activity. It follows that the machine should be so structured as to allow the most effective machine-independent programming.

The mathematical nature of programming and its separation from the machine reaches its full fruition in proofs of correctness of programming and algorithmic methods for generating a program and its proof from a specification.

In general, the rationalist view considers testing and debugging as activities that can be virtually eliminated when the programs have been properly prepared, and the often quoted "testing can never prove the absence of errors" might be supplemented with "testing is incompatible with a purely mental activity."

The activities that are most analogous to programming from the rationalist point of view are mathematics and writing. Like both these activities, programming from this perspective is essentially a one-person activity. Both the training and the work environment of the programmer should, in this view, conform to their analogy.

4.2.2 The Practitioner's Viewpoint At the other extreme from rationalism, we have empiricism:

> *Empiricism* - practice, method, or methodology relying upon direct observation or immediate experience; or precluding or excluding analysis or reflection; or employing experimentation or systematized induction as opposed to purely discursive, deductive, speculative, transcendental or dialectical procedures; or relying upon all the ways of the mind involved in inquiry [Runes].

The practitioner lives in a world of imperfect machines and languages, which are poorly and incompletely documented. He must live within specifications that call for complex systems, or he inherits programs that have bugs and must be maintained at minimum cost and cannot be redesigned.

The following from [Griswold] summarizes nicely the flavor of the practitioner's world:

> In the Spring of 1965, the first attempt was undertaken to implement SIL on another machine, the CDC 6600. At that time, there was little or no documentation of SIL, and SNOBOL4 was still under intense development. SIL was changing daily, and all parts of the system were full of bugs. The designers were hardly prepared for such an effort; they would have preferred delaying the experiment until documentation was available, and they had given some thought to how such a project should be approached. However, the opportunity was there, and the prospective implementor (or victim, as the case may be) was enthusiastic.
>
> What followed were many telephone calls, a steady flow of information through the mail, a visit or two and much suffering. The effort was justified when the first 6000 series version of SNOBOL4 began to run, if somewhat falteringly, a few months later. A solid preliminary release appeared a month or two after the corresponding 360 release, and the 6000 series implementation has kept pace ever since.

4.2.3 Semiotics - Descriptive or Prescriptive?

Semiotic - A general theory of signs and their application, especially in language; developed and systematized within Scientific Empiricism. Three branches: pragmatics, semantics, and syntax [Runes].

A general introduction to semiotics within computer science can be found in Chapter 5 of [Carberry]. Briefly, syntax is grammar, semantics is meaning, and pragmatics is ease and efficiency of use. If your program won't compile it is usually a syntax error. If it compiles but produces the wrong output, it is a semantic error. If it compiles and produces the correct output, but is unacceptably slow, that is a pragmatic problem.

It seems reasonable to expect that the documentation for a programming language system should deal with all three aspects of semiotics. The documentation must describe the statements of the language and how they are used. The effect of each statement must be given; for example, what the value of an arithmetic expression is. Finally, the documentation should give some guide to the efficient use of the language system. (Note that for the practitioner a programming language exists only as part of a system, and its semantics and, even more so, its pragmatics, are tied to the system.)

However, on each of these aspects of semiotics, our two hypothetical points of view would differ. Essentially the rationalist would expect the documentation to be the final authoritative source on all questions. Further, for the documentation to be usable, it must be well-written and of reasonable size. Thus it is easy to understand why "many academics have expressed dismay at the size of the new language," Ada [Wichmann]. (Compare the objections to Ada with the following: "If in the matters to be examined we come to a step in the series of which our understanding is not sufficiently well-able to have an intuitive cognition, we must stop short there.")

The practitioner, on the other hand, lives in a world where the documentation is often poor or incomplete, and perhaps considers the idea of using the documentation as a final arbiter, a rather Utopian notion. After all, no one has ever seen a programming language system in which the documentation is both complete and authoritative. In fact, even if prescriptive documentation were attainable, the practitioner might question its utility since it might inhibit innovation.

4.2.4 Syntax Syntax is the most fully developed of the components of semiotics, and the most widely used. The *de facto* standard for specifying syntax seems to be the Backus Naur Form, BNF, of grammar. We have discussed in [Levy 1979] and in [Joshi 1980] some of the problems with BNF. Essentially, the primary objection to BNF is that it is not natural and requires encoding of such intuitively clear ideas as precedence and associativity into unrecognizable form. (Alternative forms of grammar, such as W-

70

grammars and production rules also exist -- see e.g. [Marcotty] -- but are not widely used.)

In spite of the problems associated with BNF, it does provide a vehicle for stating the set of grammatical constructs in a language and does, therefore, allow the specification to be authoritative over implementations. Still, there are systems which implement languages for which BNF grammars exist that do not adhere to the grammar, and for which no convenient documentation exists. (In those cases, the grammar of the actually implemented language is not defined in the programmer's manual.)

Clearly such systems are usable, and when an unclear situation arises, the user can either seek the assistance of a more experienced, knowledgeable user or can experiment. One's attitude towards such systems depends, in general, on how much of a rationalist one is.

4.2.5 Semantics In syntax, it seems reasonable to expect the same form of grammar to be used both for the description of languages and for the description of programs. Whether a single form of description is applicable for semantic and pragmatic levels is unclear.

At the language level, the Vienna Definition Language, VDL [Wegner], was used to describe the semantics of PL/1. However, the VDL is an interpretive semantics and requires a (mental) execution of the VDL program to determine the computational effects of a program. (A good introduction to semantics at the language level is contained in Chapter 2 of [Aho].)

Other approaches, which to my knowledge have not been applied to complete languages, are:

- denotational or mathematical semantics (see e.g. [Tennent] or [Reynolds])

- algebraic semantics ([Goguen])

- Hoare type proof rules

Proof rule semantics of the Hoare type have been used in describing almost all of the programming language Pascal (see e.g. [Alagić]) - often excepting such difficult to formalize notions as *call by reference*. However, this occasional usage must be compared to the fairly wide acceptance of BNF.

Other approaches to semantics, which are similar to the proof rule semantics of Hoare include Dijkstra's weakest precondition [Dijkstra], and various adaptations of modal logic.

A semantic description method which would satisfy the rationalist desire for a simple and complete explication of programming remains elusive. Practitioners appear to depend increasingly on program development methodologies, documentation, and testing to define and control the meanings of programs. I think that the rationalist would prefer not to develop programs which cannot be adequately understood, and that the practitioner is satisfied with programs that generally work but have residual unidentified bugs.

4.2.6 Pragmatics Pragmatics is the least developed area of semiotics. A rationalist approach is to develop a syntax-directed method of estimating program performance. The practitioner on the other hand, generally attacks the problem via performance analysis and timing, often including elaborate instrumentation attached to the computer to provide empirical data.

4.3 The Legal Status of Software

The view of programming that prevails has consequences beyond the realm of program development or software engineering. Here I briefly comment on the implications of my concept of programming for the legal means of protecting software.

[Niblett] and [Reddien] are two readily available sources that discuss the potential methods for legal protection of software. The fact that software is not generally taken to be patentable, while programs can be copyrighted, seems to suggest that the legal system, at least, favors the rationalist view of programming.

[Nimtz] traces the history of the development of software protection. The early Patent Office position was that computer programs were not patentable because they were directed to 'mental steps'. More recently, the Software Subcommittee to the National Commission on New Technological Uses of Copyrighted Works (CONTU) has concluded that computer programs are 'works of authorship' hence subject to copyright rather than patent. A dissenting view by [Hersey] takes issue with the assertion that programs are no different from other works subject to copyright. According to Hersey: "Thus the computer program is, at different times, both a writing and a mechanical device."

[Jayachandra] also discusses the legal protection of software and concludes that "patent practitioners misconceive software as a mathematical and scientific methodology which is legally unpatentable." On the other hand, he continues that "a software program evokes a particular configuration, corresponding to the software that is being executed, in which the system performs specific functions as programmed."

Thus it would seem that a fundamental issue in the legal status of software is whether one adopts the rationalist view of programming, in which case the copyright is the appropriate form of protection, or the empiricist view of programming, in which case programs cannot be separated from the computers on which they execute.

74

4.4 Multilingual Systems

In [Freeman 1978], we argued for a multi-lingual programming system that would allow programmers to eclectically combine the best features of a variety of languages:

> Being able to write a program in a programming language suitable to expressing the solution of a problem in a straightforward manner is very desirable. String processing algorithms are easily written in SNOBOL, algebraic and vector computations are easily represented in APL, and input/output operations are effectively specified in PL/1. Since a universal language which can do all these things well is impractical at this time, it is desirable to be able to use statements from a variety of languages to express a given algorithm.

Multilingual systems are essential if we are to encourage varieties of programming method and style in the development of application systems. If the main thesis of this chapter is correct, then the accommodation of a range of programming languages and styles within a single project is a requisite for the most efficient use of a variety of talents.

Although the ability to best use the capabilities of different people is the primary reason within the central theme of this chapter, there are at least two other important reasons for multilingual systems. First, such systems would enhance the reuse of

75

existing software modules, since the reason for new software development is often the choice of language. In a multi-lingual system, any project could use any modules developed by any other language, and important savings would result. Second, the availability of multilingual systems would encourage the development of new languages and the addition of new features to existing languages, since language compatibility would not be the factor that it now is. A multilingual system, because it can accommodate different languages, can certainly accommodate greater variability in successive standards of the same base language without the often restrictive requirement of upward compatibility of the successive language versions.

Finally, the importance of multilingual systems is likely to increase significantly as the size of systems increases. Then just as the ability to combine separate compilations speeds development, the ability to write in the language most natural to a particular aspect of the application would have the same effect.

An approach which appears to be similar is described in [Gyllstrom] where a Universal Compiling System (UCS) provides a multilingual approach:

> The user benefits from the universality requirement of UCS because the execution environment is the same for all programs written in the UCS languages. This allows and encourages

multiple languages within an application or program.

4.5 Simplicity[2]

> Intellectual control is the key to orderly development. -
> H.D. Mills

Since software engineering deals with the construction of man-made programs, the attributes of these programs are determined by the people who construct them and their methods and approach. For a fixed initial cost, there is a trade off of simplicity vs. functionality which should follow the general form of Figure 4.1. One is forced to choose between added function and greater simplicity. Achieving simple and understandable programs and machines requires a conscious selection of simplicity as a design criterion and a concern for the choice of structure to achieve the simplicity.

The tradeoff curve of simplicity vs. functionality may be shifted by an added initial investment. Some of the initial costs that can shift the curve, achieving, for example, more functionality with the

---

[2] This section is based on [Levy 1981]. That paper contains many more examples than the two presented in this section.

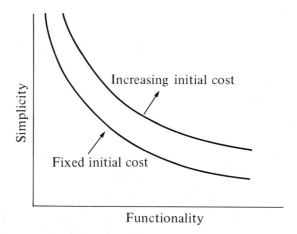

Figure 4.1 Tradeoff of Simplicity for Functionality

same level of simplicity are:

- design studies

- prototyping

- additional equipment

- design architecture

While simplicity is hard to characterize, some of the factors that provide simplicity are consistency and the hiding of irrelevant detail. What follows are some examples.

4.5.1 Hiding Irrelevant Detail In circuit theory it is well known that three terminals A, B, and C in a network with a purely resistive impedance between pairs of terminals can be replaced with either of the two subnetworks known as wye and delta shown in

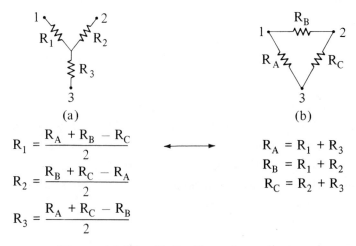

(a)   (b)

$$R_1 = \frac{R_A + R_B - R_C}{2}$$

$$R_2 = \frac{R_B + R_C - R_A}{2}$$

$$R_3 = \frac{R_A + R_C - R_B}{2}$$

$$R_A = R_1 + R_3$$
$$R_B = R_1 + R_2$$
$$R_C = R_2 + R_3$$

Figure 4.2 Wye-Delta Transformations

Figure 4.2. Transformations between the form of Figure 4.2a and Figure 4.2b are called wye-delta transformations. Given a network of resistors between terminals A,B, and C, the problem is to reduce it to a simple wye. Two additional elementary transformations are needed:

- replacing a series connection of two resistors with a single resistor

- replacing a parallel connection of resistors with a single resistor.

4.5.2 Consistency In the PDP-11 all instructions that operate on data, as a side effect, will set condition codes according to the results of the indicated operation. For instance, the operation
       DEC A
decrements the contents of location A by one. If the resulting value in location A is zero, a condition code reflecting this is automatically set.

Unfortunately, the setting of these condition codes is often incorrect. One can see this by observing that the semantics of *DEC B* (decrement the contents of location B by one) are not the same as the semantics of *SUB #1,B* (subtract one from the contents of location B) The *DEC* does not change the carry bit (condition code) while the *SUB* does. Hence the sequence
       DEC B
       BHI L
may result in different action from the sequence
       SUB #1,B
       BHI L
depending on how the carry bit is set before the *DEC* instruction since the conditional branch instruction *BHI* is activated when the condition codes indicate an unsigned result that is greater than zero.

This sort of inconsistency can lead to increased complexity in writing compilers that generate *good* code as well as lead to code which is hard to understand and maintain.

But there is usually a price to be paid for consistency -- *performance.* For instance, if we design a machine with the philosophy that all instructions are atomic - that is, non-interruptable - then we pay a price for including a block move operation in our instruction set. Of course, it might be more reasonable to allow block moves to be interruptable (as in the IBM 370) but that would violate consistency. Clearly, in an atomic instruction set interrupts cannot be serviced during a move. Furthermore, to achieve consistency specific implementation techniques may not be used; for example, pipelining of the instruction stream is stopped by an atomic block move instruction.

4.6 Summing Up Simplicity

To the extent that there is a software crisis, it is self-induced. We have tried to build systems whose complexity overwhelms us, because there is often a tradeoff between simplicity and performance.

But the choice is also influenced by factors which are difficult to quantify. How comfortable are we with software - or hardware - that adds features but increases complexity? Different people will have different ideas, but the rationalist will tend to favor the simple and consistent solutions, while the empiricist will tend to favor functionality.

4.7 Conclusion

In the natural sciences different views of reality can be tested against the 'objective reality,' and a consensus achieved as to the more effective way to describe the world. Programming is a man-made activity -- programming languages and systems, the programming environment, are all synthetic -- and can, therefore, be adapted to our concept of what programming is. The formal education and training of new computer scientists can also be made to conform. On the other hand, the deeper psychological aspects of programmer personality and philosophical outlook are not, and *should not be*, adaptable to any preconception of programming.

A more careful study of programming concepts and milieu and their relation to personality types is needed. (It is interesting to take authors and systems with which one is familiar and try to identify where in the rationalist/empiricist spectrum they lie.) However, such a study should not alter the conclusion that programming is, and should be, different for different people. What is needed are programming milieus that allow greater flexibility.

Earlier in this century, children used to be forced to use their right hands to write, and left-handedness was neither encouraged nor tolerated. We have since learned to accept the physiological

Conclusion

differences of left-handedness. Our view of programming must be
similarly broadened.

Chapter 5

Software Engineering

In this chapter, I first survey the concerns of software engineering. Next, since the development of methodology has been one of the major concerns of software engineering, I discuss the role of a design methodology and show how the method of metaprogramming, presented in Chapter 3, compares with some other methods. Finally, since software economics is one of the major driving forces behind the method of metaprogramming, I discuss it briefly. However, the main discussion of software economics is presented in Chapters 7-9.

The tar pit of software engineering will continue to be sticky for a long time to come. One may expect the human race to continue attempting systems just within or just beyond our reach; and software systems are perhaps the most intricate and most complex of man's handiwork. The management of this complex craft will demand our best use of new languages and systems, our best adaptation of proven engineering management methods, liberal doses of common sense, and a God-given humility to recognize our fallibility and limitations. [Brooks]

When group size exceeds five or more people, most of the time is spent on communication with the group members about what they're doing and very little is actually spent in coding or developing systems. We need a greater understanding of the process of writing such systems in order to be able to rapidly produce large scale natural language understanding systems. [Waltz]

Programming is difficult because it is very complex and very changeable. Mastering the complexity requires the combined efforts of many people whose joint activities must be coordinated. The changeability both of requirements and of technology makes planning difficult because of the large uncertainty. These problems led to the evolution of software engineering as a discipline for managing programming.

Software Engineering

Software engineering is relatively new, having its origins in the mid 60's when the problems of constructing large software systems became apparent to all. Such systems were often late, poorly constructed, and much more expensive than predicted. The concern of software engineering is the construction of *large* programs.

As [Brooks] has noted, the problem of software engineering is that it encompasses both management and programming, but the management of software is different from more traditional forms of management and the programming of large scale software requires different concerns than the programming of small projects.

The Mythical Man-Month deals with the failure of traditional management methodologies to control software systems development and some of the special properties of software that contribute to that failure. It is particularly concerned with large systems whose costs both in manpower and time exceed those planned. I would agree with [Brooks] on the problems confronting the software world, and even with his diagnosis of their symptoms, and this book describes my approach.

I begin this chapter with an outline of the major problems of software and a list of the major topics of software engineering. A synthesis of software engineering approaches to the development of programs is called a *methodology*, and I discuss software methodologies, in general, and propose a specific methodology. The methodology described involves choices, whose basis is ultimately economic, with due allowance being made for our inability to predict accurately both costs and benefits. The economics of the choices is the concern of Chapters 7-9, so this chapter concludes with some comments on the relationship of software economics to software engineering and a brief discussion of software costs.

5.1 Software Engineering: Problems

Some of the major problems in the development of software are:

Schedule
: Developing software on schedule is a continuing problem, typified by Brook's Law: *Adding manpower to a late software project makes it later.*

Problems of scale
: The distinction between small and large programs.

Conceptual integrity
: Keeping a design elegant [1]

---

[1] "Simplicity and straightforwardness proceed from conceptual integrity. Every part must reflect the same philosophies and the same balancing of desiderata. Every part must use the same techniques in syntax and analogous notions in semantics. Ease of use, then, dictates unity of design, conceptual integrity." [Brooks]

Software Engineering

Load balancing	What do implementors do while the system is being designed?
Specifications	Assuring correctness Assuring style and readability
Organization	Establishing an organization which can work effectively for a common purpose.
Difficulty of estimating	How much should it cost?
Control of resources	How much is it costing?
Documentation	In the large - producing the project documents for the customer and for the management of the project. In the small - Producing commentary on the programs.
Testing and validation	Getting the bugs out.

The following are the central concerns of software engineering [2]:

---

[2] These topics were covered in a graduate course on software engineering which the author gave in the Department of Mathematics and Computer Science at Ben Gurion University in the spring of 1984.

Also, one aspect of software engineering training that seems to be generally agreed is that practical experience is a *sine qua non*. An important

88

Software Engineering: Problems

Project management	General principles of management [3].
Software economics	Methods for trading off different factors of production in software costs.
Software design	Methodologies currently used in developing software [4].

---

aspect of the software engineering course was a class project for learning and demonstrating the principles of the subject.

[3] Speaking of software problems, [Shooman] writes: "Many of the problems stem from an unrealistic view of what it takes to construct the set of programs - the computer software - which is required to instruct the computer hardware in performing the necessary computations. In order to improve the record to date, we must better understand the software development process and learn how to estimate and trade off the time, manpower, and dollars needed to produce software. An important goal is to learn how to initially estimate and subsequently measure the quality, reliability, and cost of the product."

[4] Software design is included because the essence of design is making those choices which restrict successive choices. In the case of software these choices are often discussed in the literature as *separation of concerns* and *abstraction*. However, *separation of concerns* is just *division of labor* or *specialization* in management terminology. Similarly, *abstraction* is remarkably close to the management concept of *delegation*. It is arguable to what extent those choices are technical or managerial, but they must be the concern of software engineering.

89

Software testing   Testing and validation of large programs [5].

Tools   Software tools that are used for the development, testing, and management of software systems [Kernighan].

Productivity   Problem of achieving greater programmer productivity.

Other topics which are prominent in the software engineering literature are:

- Software specifications

- Standards

- Maintenance

- Documentation

- Effective communication

---

[5] Software testing is included primarily because it seems to be an otherwise ignored topic in computer science curricula, and because it has a major impact on the management of large software projects.

- Programmer training

- Human factors issues

- Legal aspects

- Make or buy decisions

- Rapid prototyping

- Correctness

- Programming environments

- Software reliability

And, surely, even that list is not exhaustive!

5.2 Design Methodology

An important goal of software engineering is the evolution of a design methodology. We have discussed in Chapter 3 what the general characteristics of a software design method are.

Most of the software development methodologies are based on a life cycle concept that proceeds through the following stages:

1. requirements analysis

2. specification

3. design

4. coding

5. test and integration

6. maintenance

Design methodologies are then defined which proceed from a well-defined specification and cover both the design and coding phases.

In this approach, much detail is fixed early in the specifications, on the assumption that that detail is needed for a good design. There are at least two major flaws with this approach:

1. The assumption that having a detailed specification will allow a good design is not borne out in practice. This has led to Brooks' rule on system design: *Build one to throw away* [Brooks].

2. Since maintenance often includes changes in requirements or specifications, these changes may cause significant variations in the design, especially if the design is sensitive to details in the specification.

5.2.1 A Specific Methodology I believe a restructuring of the software life cycle is needed in which only the requirements needed to construct a prototype are fixed using the method of *metaprogramming* as described in Chapter 3.

Another approach described in the literature [Basili] that seems to be in the spirit of Brooks' Law proceeds as follows:

1. Formulate an initial overall design

2. Using a project control list of design tasks, choose a task and

    a. design

    b. implement

    c. analyze

The analysis may then result in new tasks being added to the list of pending tasks [6].

Another methodology I like is that of [Donelon]. It starts with the development of a user manual as the first stage. Once the user manual is defined, it helps determine some key decisions. In the next stage, the top level descriptions in the user manual are utilized

---

[6] This approach is known as *planning* in the literature of artificial intelligence, where plans are formulated and then subgoals are elaborated. See e.g. Chapter 8 of [Rich].

to develop a project plan from which estimates and schedules are determined. Note that this methodology also fixes the overall structure before concentrating on the details.

Note that in our methodology the project control list of design tasks will be heavily weighted with tool construction activities.

The methodology described, entailing a restructuring of the software life cycle, has management implications, since it is clear that detailed planning and the concomitant contractual obligations cannot be undertaken until the prototype is completed. However, the earlier setting of plans in the currently envisioned life cycle is illusory since the plans are almost never realized [7].

5.2.2 Rationale

> Every problem that I solved became a method to solve other problems.
>
> - Descartes

---

[7] One could, of course, proceed with the current software life cycle, keeping the prototype construction transparent to the customer. This has the disadvantage that the customer is not able to use the application generators in setting the specifications.

Design Methodology

Here are the general principles that underlie my methodology:

1. *It defers decisions.* Late *binding time* is desirable where better information or insight may be subsequently available. From an economic point of view, decisions taken early have the greatest associated cost because:

    - Most of the work is based on them.

    - Hence,the cost of reversing wrong decisions is largest.

    - If no subsequent work is done on the basis of an early decision, then that decision should have been deferred because the effort expended in making that decision could have been expended elsewhere.

2. *It factors out variable portions of the work.* This is the basic idea of *data independence* that occurs both in expert systems, discussed in Section 2.3, and in [Codd]'s relational data base work [8].

---

[8] The motivations for relational database are:
  - data independence
  - communicability
  - set processing

    [Codd]

3. *It automates the repetitive part of the work.* This saves time initially and also helps ensure consistency and correctness [Levinson].

4. *It allows the creation of a suitable notation appropriate to the application.* This facilitates communication [Levy 1985].

5.3 Software Economics

5.3.1 Why Software Economics? Software engineering attempts to develop programs in a well organized manner. As shown in Figure 5.1, software engineering encompasses both a technical aspect, programming, and a managerial component. Both the management and technical components are affected by the choices implied by the component labeled *software economics.*

A major objective of software engineering is to allow the system *architect,* or software project manager, to provide the system with a unity of structure that is characterized by *top-down* design while allowing the concurrency of development of other methodologies [9].

---

[9] The basic rationalist approach, as described in Descartes' *Discourse on Method,* for example, is a goal-oriented problem decomposition technique. This contrasts with the *bottom-up* approach illustrated by the quote from [Griswold] in Chapter 3.

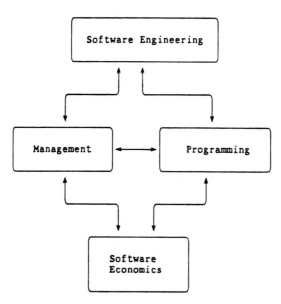

Figure 5.1. Software Engineering, Programming, and Software Economics

There is an inherent tension between the desire for an orderly development methodology in which each decision is taken at a time determined solely by the logic of the evolving system, and the need to layout a detailed system schedule, including integration and test, before major elements of the architecture have been defined [10]. In a fully developed system of software economics, it would be possible to evaluate each activity of system design, and to provide a quantitative basis for the decisions that are taken, and to determine where in the development cycle they are made.

Economic techniques which establish a foundation for tradeoffs in decisions about system development are quite different from techniques for costing software which analyze the development and design processes based on historic data of questionable validity.

5.3.2 Estimating Software Costs

5.3.2.1 Overview We typically estimate the cost of software by extrapolating from historic data. Since the data are known to be full of contradictions and to contain wide variations, different models try to account for these discrepancies.

[Mohanty] in a recent survey has written:

Since 1965, several models have been proposed for estimating

---

[10] "... a great deal of the success of a project will depend upon the improvisational skill and the resources available to the technical managers. The perils of insufficient effort being devoted to decision making are obvious, but it is argued that there is a balance between the extreme of 'overdeciding' and maintaining the flexibility to the unforeseen." [Corbato]

software costs. Today, there are more than 20 such cost models. But, it is highly unlikely that any two models will estimate the same cost for a given project. We also observe that, even today, almost no model can estimate the true cost of software with any degree of certainty. Analysis reveals that these variations are influenced by many factors and the quantization of these factors by the user of the models.

He then gives an analysis of a medium size, 36,000 line software system for which the estimated costs using the models varied from a low of $362,500 to a high of $2,766,667 [11]. Since many of the models also estimate development time, these were also obtained, and ranged from 13.77 to 25.8 months. (As a uniform basis for estimating costs, programming salaries were estimated at $50,000 per burdened staff-year.)

We can get a rough estimate of the range of program cost by assuming a programmer productivity rate of 2,500 to 5,000 lines per staff-year and calculating that 36,000 lines will take between 7.2 and 14.4 staff years with a resultant cost of $360,000 to $720,000. We

---

[11] Note that in a real estimate the number of lines of program are not known in advance and might, therefore, add considerably to the variance of the estimates.

might then improve that estimate of the cost by deciding how
difficult the specific programming project was. The actual models
try to refine the estimates by dividing the programming task into
different levels of difficulty and assigning different productivity
factors to these tasks.

Estimates of project duration, or staffing profile, are derived
from similar data by assuming an equation relating the size of the
project to the staffing. These equations attempt to account for the
well-known fact that people and time are not interchangeable: you
cannot generally halve the project duration by doubling the staff.

In the next subsection we shall look at one of the cost models in
more detail.

5.3.2.2 The Putnam Model [Putnam] has expounded a model of
software development in which the cumulative staff effort, y, on a
project is given by a Rayleigh distribution

$$y(t) = K(1 - e^{-at^2}) \tag{1}$$

where K = total effort required in staff-months

$$a = \frac{1}{t_d{}^2}$$

t_d = time until project staffing reaches a peak

The derivation of Equation 1 is as follows, [Parr]: Let $y(t)$ be the
effort expended up to time, t, and let $p(t)$ be the *pace* at which work
is done. Then the rate of progress, dy/dt, is proportional to the

product of *p(t)* and the effort remaining to be expended:

$$\frac{dy}{dt} = p(K - y) \tag{2}$$

Integrating Equation 2 with the boundary condition *y(0)* = 0 yields:

$$y = K(1 - e^{-\int p \, dt}) \tag{3}$$

If we assume a linear learning curve, then:

$$p(t) = at \tag{4}$$

Substituting Equation 4 in Equation 3 and integrating, we have

$$y = K(1 - e^{-\frac{at^2}{2}}) \tag{5a}$$

$$\frac{dy}{dt} = Kate^{-\frac{at^2}{2}} \tag{5b}$$

Equation 1, which is the basic equation relating project profile to total effort, has the additional parameter, *a*, which can easily be shown to satisfy the equation,

$$a = \frac{1}{t_d{}^2}$$

One can then determine the maximum acceptable, *a*, by limiting the (normalized) rate of growth of the staff.

[Putnam] further obtains an empirical equation:

$$Kt^4 = constant \tag{6}$$

to account for the observation that people and time are not interchangeable.

The fact that people and time are not interchangeable is an instance of a more general economic principle that resources are not interchangeable. If the two resources used to produce an item are capital and labor, and if the supply of capital is fixed, then at some point the marginal productivity of each worker - the quantity that the worker produces - will be less. In fact, if sufficient additional labor is added the marginal productivity may be negative: some workers may get in the way of other workers, reducing their productivity. In general, we may expect the marginal productivity of labor to initially increase, then level off, subsequently decline, and, finally, become negative.

While the [Putnam] model is more analytic than most software costing models, it is certainly not a unified model and combines empirical eata with the Rayleigh nurve in quite an *ad hoc* manner [13]. [Parr], for example, has criticized the basic model. Other general models develop a somewhat different project profile, and the arguments for one model over another are not convincing.

---

[13] Most software cost models are purely empirical and are derived by fitting some assumed polynomial form to a collection of cost data.

My basic disagreement with these models is that they try to predict the costs, in time and effort, of software on the assumption that the new software will be developed in much the same way as the old software. If our assumption that software development needs a radical restructuring is correct, then the validity of any models which massage historic data is dubious. In Chapter 7, I present some new software costing models as alternatives.

5.3.2.3 Other Models Without considering the details of other models, their general approach is to calculate

$$M = f_1(p_1, p_2, \cdots, p_n)$$
$$T = f_2(p_1, p_2, \cdots, p_n)$$

where M is the number of staff-months of effort, and T is the project duration. $p_1, \cdots, p_n$ are parameters chosen in an attempt to get a good fit to past historic data and may include objective data such as lines of source code, number of files, number of transactions, and subjective factors such as complexity of algorithms.

Chapter 6

AWK - A Prototyping Language

AWK is an interpretive programming language, which makes it useful for prototyping. Primary applications of AWK are information retrieval, report writing, and data manipulation.

AWK is often used as a special purpose information processing language, many of whose capabilities are easily accessible to non-programmers. We present it as a programming language with added capabilities, particularly useful for metaprogramming.

After presenting a tutorial overview of the language, I give a small metaprogramming example of the development of a data validation program. In this example the model is a concise specification describing the data to be validated and the error messages if the data are not validated.

AWK (named for its developers, Al Aho, Peter Weinberger, and Brian Kernighan) is a programming language and system with many characteristics that make it a convenient problem-solving tool [1]. Important characteristics of the language are its ability to process files, refer to input records and their fields, and match patterns on these items. Typically, an input record is one line of an input file, and fields are delimited by white space.

The pattern expressions used by AWK are similar to those used in other commands of the UNIX system [Unix], [2], and the control structures are similar to other high level algorithmic languages such as C or Pascal. AWK is also similar to interpretive languages in that no declarations are used.

Typical applications of AWK make use of these features. Among such applications are information retrieval and report writing, especially on record oriented input. Another use of AWK is for data manipulation, or validation, exploiting the pattern matching features.

AWK is often thought of as a sequence of pattern statements, in which each action is preceded by a guard. Thus the program

---

[1] An earlier version of this chapter appeared in [Levy 1983].
[2] UNIX is a registered trademark of Bell Laboratories.

```
/AWK/ {
        print NR
}
```

when run against a file will produce a list of the line numbers of all
the lines in which the sequence of letters AWK appears.

6.1 Hello World

Each AWK program consists of three parts:

- a <BEGIN section>

- a <pattern statement section>

- an <END section>.

We will start with the <BEGIN section> which is run before
any input records are processed. The <END section> is run after
all input records have been processed, and the <pattern section>
is data driven. The following program prints *Hello World!*:

```
BEGIN{
        print "Hello World!"
        exit
}
```

106

This program is entirely contained in the <BEGIN section> and therefore is run before any data are read. (Since AWK programs are normally terminated by the end of input, the *exit* is needed here to cause the program to end.)

NOTE: Brackets, {}, are used to define the limits of the sequence of statements associated with the <BEGIN section>. They are similar to the bracketing pairs of words used in other block structured languages, such as *do ... od* and *begin ... end.*

A more elaborate example is the following AWK version of the Euclidean algorithm to compute the greatest common divisor of a pair of numbers. (The greatest common divisor of a pair of numbers is the largest integer that divides each of the numbers.) The following is a program for the Euclidean algorithm:

```
BEGIN{
    i = 75 ; j = 30
    while( i != j ) {
        if ( i > j )
            i -= j
        else
            j -= i
    }
    print "The greatest common divisor" \
        " of 75 and 30 is " i
```

107

```
        exit
    }
```

NOTE: The statement

```
    i -= j
```

is equivalent to the statement

```
    i = i - j
```

This type of construct is used in Algol 68 and C.

NOTE: AWK is an interpretive language. There are no declarations, the types of variables being inferred by the AWK processor. Further, a variable may take on different types of values within the same program.

NOTE: More than one statement may appear on a line if the statements are separated by semicolons.

NOTE: Statements may be continued on succeeding lines by terminating a line with a '\'. When a quoted string is to be continued on a succeeding line, it must be treated as the concatenation of component substrings, since '\' may not be used within a quoted string.

The output of the above program is:

```
The greatest common divisor of 75 and 30 is 15.
```

In the preceding program, the data on which the program operates are built in. More generally programs operate on records in files. Unless otherwise specified:

- A record is a single line in a file.

- Fields within a record are strings of non-white space characters separated by white space characters, i.e. blanks or tabs. (Both record and field delimiters can be specified by the user.)

- $i refers to the ith field of a record when i is one or more.

- $0 refers to the whole input record.

The following program is an AWK implementation of the Euclidean algorithm that computes the greatest common divisors of pairs of numbers. The data are stored as pairs of numbers, one pair on each line of the input data file. Each pair of numbers thus constitutes two fields of a record.

```
{
 arg1 = $1 ; arg2 = $2
 while (arg1 != arg2) {
     if (arg1 > arg2)
         arg1 -= arg2
     else
         arg2 -= arg1
     }
 print "The greatest common divisor of " $1 \
     " and " $2 " is " arg1
```

Given the following input data:

75	30
24	60
360	224

the following output will be generated:

```
The greatest common divisor of 75 and 30 is 15.
The greatest common divisor of 24 and 60 is 12.
The greatest common divisor of 360 and 224 is 8.
```

Notice that this program does not have a <BEGIN section> since there is no computation required before processing the first record. In general, the <BEGIN section> is used as the initialization part of the AWK program. Correspondingly, there is an <END section> when some computation is required after all records have been processed.

The following is a program to compute the root mean square of a set of numbers:

```
# A program to compute the square root of the
# sum of the squares of a set of numbers.
# The set of numbers is provided as input -
# one number to a record.
#
# NR is the current record number. In the END
# section it is number of records.

BEGIN{
    sum_of_squares = 0
    }
    {
        sum_of_squares += $1 * $1
    }
```

```
END{
    root_mean_square = sqrt(sum_of_squares / NR)
    print root_mean_square
    }
```

NOTE: Comments are used in the preceding program. A # is a comment marker: anything following it on a line in the program file is treated as comment.

In the preceding program, the <BEGIN section> initializes **sum_of_squares** to 0. (AWK initializes all numeric variables to 0, so the <BEGIN section> is not really needed here.) The fifth line of the program, ignoring blank and comment lines, is run on each record and adds the square of the first field of the record to **sum_of_squares**. Since each input number is stored in a separate record and constitutes the first (and only) field of that record, the effect is to add up the squares af all numbers. Finally, the <END section> uses a built-in AWK variable, **NR**, and a built-in AWK function, **sqrt()**, to compute the **root_mean_square**. The **root_mean_square** of a set of items is defined as the square root of the sum of the squares of the items divided by the number of items. **NR** is a built-in AWK variable that is a count of the number of input records encountered. When processing the ith record the value of **NR** is i. Thus in the <END section>, **NR** is a count of the number of records. In this program it is, therefore, a count of the number of items. `Sqrt()` is the square root function.

6.2 Some AWK Syntax

The basic AWK syntax can be summarized in the following Backus-Naur Form, BNF, [Carberry et al] or [Levy], definition:

<Program>   ::= <BEGIN section>
           <pattern statement section>
           <END section>

<BEGIN section>   ::= BEGIN {
           <statement list>
           } |
           empty

<pattern statement section> ::= <pattern statement list> |
           empty

<END section>   ::= END {
           <statement list>
           } |
           empty

<statement>	::=	"A statement in a C-like syntax"

<pattern statement>	::=	<pattern>	{
		<statement list>	}	
		<pattern>	

The English language rendition of this grammar is that a program consists of a <BEGIN section> followed by a <pattern section> followed by an <END section>. (The <>'s denote syntactic categories, ::= is read "is defined as," and | is read as "or".)

- A <BEGIN section> consists of the word BEGIN (all caps) followed by a list of statements surrounded by braces, or a <BEGIN section> is empty.

- An <END section> consists of the word END (all caps) followed by a list of statements surrounded by braces, or a <END section> is empty.

- The <pattern statement section> consists of a sequence of <pattern statement>'s, or may be empty. If the <pattern statement section> is not empty, then each <pattern

114

statement> consists of a <pattern> followed by a <statement list> enclosed in braces, or a <pattern statement> is just a <pattern>, and the default action is to print the record.

- A <statement list> is a sequence of one or more <statement>'s. This could be described by the BNF rule:

<statement   ::= <statement list>
                                                  <statement> |
                                                  <statement>

Similarly, <pattern statement list> can be cast in BNF form.

6.3 Patterns

AWK may be thought of as a pattern-driven language in which the standard paradigm is a sequence of pattern-action pairs. In this view of AWK each pattern acts as a *guard* for the statement following it. The three types of patterns that AWK comprehends are:

1.   regular expression patterns

2.   arithmetic patterns

3.   range patterns.

AWK - A Prototyping Language

Regular expression pattern specification in AWK is similar to regular pattern expression specification in other UNIX commands and is based on the specification of a regular expression defining the set of strings that constitute the pattern. The pattern is delimited by pairs of /'s. Within a pattern, most symbols denote themselves [3], with the exception of the special symbols to be described. Thus /a/ denotes the pattern consisting of the single letter *a*, and /ab/ denotes denotes the pattern consisting of the sequence of two letters *ab*.

The following symbols have special meanings within regular expression patterns:

---

[3] More precisely, most symbols denote the singleton set containing that symbol.

Patterns

Symbol	Meaning	Examples
|	alternation	a|b means 'a' or 'b'
		ab|cd means 'ab' or 'cd'
+	one or more	a+ means one or more 'a's
?	zero or one	a? means zero or one 'a's
*	zero or more	a* means zero or more 'a's
[...]	pattern class	[ab] means 'a' or 'b'
		[aeiou] means any vowel
		[a-z] means any lower case letter
^	beginning anchor	^[a-z] means a pattern
$	ending anchor	[0-9]$ means a pattern
		ending with a
		decimal digit

^ [a-zA-Z][a-zA-Z0-9]* is a pattern whose first symbol is a letter and whose succeeding symbols, if any, are letters or digits.

Recall that a <pattern statement> is a <pattern expression> followed by a <statement list>. The <pattern expression> may consist solely of a pattern in which case the <pattern expression> matches *iff* [4] $0, the entire record, satisfies the pattern. A <pattern expression> may also be formed using the relational operators:

==	equals
!=	does not equal
>	is greater than
>=	is greater than or equal to
<	is less than
<=	is less than or equal to

or the pattern operators:

~	matches

Patterns

!~   does not match

The <pattern expression> $1 ~ /a/ is true whenever field #1 contains an *a*. The pattern expression $1 ~ /^a/ is true *iff* field #1 starts with an *a*, and $1 ~ /^a$/ is true *iff* field #1 is just the letter *a*. Other examples are:

$2 !~ /1|a/   true if field #2 contains
                               neither a *1* nor an *a*

$3 ~ /^this$|^that$/   true if field #3 is exactly
                               this or *that*

<pattern expression>'s may also be composed into more complicated <pattern expression>'s by using the Boolean connectives *and, or,* and *not* denoted by the symbols &&, ||, and !, respectively.

     (x ~ /a/ || x ~ /b/) && x !~ /c/

---

[4] *iff* is an abbreviation of the phrase *if and only if*.

is a pattern that is true *iff* x is a string which has an a or a b in its string value and does not have a c in its string value.

6.4 More of the Language

The following are built-in constructs in AWK:

- FS - A built-in variable that defines the field separator.

- substr(...) - The substring function. Substr(s,m,n) gives the n character substring of s starting at position m. If s is a number its print image is used:

      substr(123456789,3,4) is 3456

If the third argument is omitted, the result is the substring of s starting at position m; i.e. the rest of the string:

      substr("123456789",3) is 3456789

- index - index(s,t) is a function whose arguments are strings, and whose value is the starting position of the leftmost occurrence of t in s. If t is not a substring of s, then index(s,t) is 0.

      index("Kernighan","nigh") is 4.

- split - split(x,y,z) assigns the fields of the string x to successive elements of the array y using the character z as the string x field separator.

- for - the iterative construct in AWK. Like the C language construct, it has three arguments: the first argument is an initialization, the second argument is a termination condition, and the third argument specifies an increment.

```
for(i = 1 ; i <= NF ; i++)
    print i, $i
```

prints each field of a record preceded by the number of the field. (NF is a built-in AWK variable which takes on the value of the number of fields in the current record.)

There is much more to the AWK language than what has been covered here, but the presentation has concentrated on those parts of AWK needed to understand the example program generator.

6.5 EXAMPLE - A Data Validator

6.5.1 Background of the Example During the academic year 1983-84, I was teaching at Ben Gurion University of the Negev in Israel. During the fall semester I taught artificial intelligence and during the spring semester, software engineering. (In fact, this book had its start while I was teaching.) In the spring semester we developed a prototype of an expert system shell for advisement systems; i.e. we developed a set of tools that would be useful for any advice-giving system. The domain of our prototype was student advisement including:

- checking a proposed course schedule

- checking graduation requirements

- recommending courses to students

The expert system shell included a screen package, forms, a primitive natural language query interface, a report writer and other utilities. One of the utilities provided was a validation checker to assure that the records used by the system were accurate syntactically. Since there would be a variety of different file types, it was desirable that the validation checker be generated from a concise specification to minimize the amount of programming needed. In this way, each new syntax checker could be produced by the same generator.

In the next section are described some of the validation criteria that the generator could handle. Following this I will develop the AWK program that produces the validation checker from the specification.

EXAMPLE - A Data Validator

6.5.2 The Specification of the Validation Criteria The validation criteria to be described are field validations. We assume that each record consists of a sequence of fields separated by *tabs*. (The complete validator also included cross-field validations, record validations, and validations of the overall structure of the file.) The four types of validations performed by the validator described here are:

- Check that a field matches a given regular expression.

- Check that the contents of a field is one of a finite set of strings.

- Check that the length of a field is within fixed limits.

- Check that a field is an integer in a given range.

The specification will consist of a set of lines, each line containing four fields. The first field determines the type of validation check; F in the first field says that the check is a field validation. The second field is an integer specifying to which field the validation applies. The third field describes the specification for the given field as follows:

- R(x) - where x is a regular expression, specifies that the field must match the regular expression.

123

- S(x) - where x is a list of strings, separated by commas, specifies that the field must be one of the given strings.

- L(m,n) - where m and n are integers, specifies that the length of the field must lie in the range m..n, inclusive.

- N(m,n) - where m and n are integers, specifies that the value field must be an integer in the range $m..n$ inclusive.

The fourth field is an error message which will be printed out if the field in question fails to satisfy the validation criteria.

An example specification is:

```
F    1    R(a)              Must contain an 'a'
F    2    S(alpha,beta) Must be alpha or beta
F    3    L(4,7)            Must have length between 4 and 7
F    4    N(5,8)            Must be integer between 5 and 8
```

6.5.3 The Generator The following is the complete AWK program to implement the validation generator described in the preceding section:

EXAMPLE - A Data Validator

```
BEGIN{
   FS = "\t" # specifies a tab as a field separator
   cs = "# "  # comment start
   ce = ""    # comment end
   }


$1 == "F" {
                           # preparse
   field = $2
   type = substr($3,1,1)
   content = substr($3,3,length($3)-3)
   print cs "field = " field ce
   print cs "type = " type ce
   print cs "content = " content ce

   if (type == "R"){
      print "$" field " !~ /" content "/ {"
      print " print \"line #\" NR \" field #" field " - " $4 "\"
      print " }"
      }

   if (type == "L"){
      comma = index(content,",")
      print cs "comma = " comma ce
      lolim = substr(content,1,comma - 1)
```

```
    hilim = substr(content, comma + 1)
    print cs "lolim = " lolim "; hilim = " hilim ce
    print "length($" field ") < " lolim " || length($" field ") > "
    print "        print \"line #\" NR \" field #" field " - " $4 "\""
    print "        }"
    }


if (type == "N"){
    comma = index(content,",")
    print cs "comma = " comma ce
    lolim = substr(content,1,comma - 1)
    hilim = substr(content, comma + 1)
    print cs "lolim = " lolim "; hilim = " hilim ce
    print "$" field " !~ /[0-9][0-9]*/ || $" field " < " lolim \
          " || $" field " > " hilim " {"
    print "        print \"line #\" NR \" field #" field " - " $4 "\""
    print "        }"
    }


if (type == "S"){
            n = split(content,check,",")
    pat = "^" check[1] "$"
    for(i=2;i<=n;i++){
        pat = pat "|^" check[i] "$"
        }
```

126

```
   print cs "pat = " pat ce
   print "$" field " !~ /" pat "/ {"
   print "        print \"line #\" NR \" field #" field " - " $4 "\"
   print "        }"
   }
   }
END{
   print ""
   }
```

Since the four sections of the code are fairly similar, dealing with the four types of field specification, I will discuss only the L case. For convenience of discussion the relevant part of the code is reproduced below:

```
BEGIN{
   FS = ""   # field separator is a tab
   cs = "# "  # comment start
   ce = ""    # comment end
   }
```

```
$1 == "F" {
                            # preparse
    field = $2
    type = substr($3,1,1)
    content = substr($3,3,length($3)-3)
    print cs "field = " field ce
    print cs "type = " type ce
    print cs "content = " content ce

    if (type == "L"){
        comma = index(content,",")
        print cs "comma = " comma ce
        lolim = substr(content,1,comma - 1)
        hilim = substr(content, comma + 1)
        print cs "lolim = " lolim "; hilim = " hilim ce
        print "length($" field ") < " lolim
        print "        print \"line #\" NR \" field #" field " - " $4 "\"
        print "        }"
        }


    }
END{
    print ""
    }
```

EXAMPLE - A Data Validator

The first statement in the <BEGIN section> of the program initializes the field separator, FS, to be a tab, rather than any white space. The next two statements specify the comment delimiters that are to be generated by the generator. Since, in this case, the generated program is to be an AWK program the start of comment is a '#'. For completeness I have also specified a comment terminator as a null string, although it is not needed for the generated AWK program. Other languages do require comment terminators.

The main body of the program is preceded by the guard expression which checks that the first field is the letter 'F' so that what is being specified is a field specification. The next three lines, set to the value of the variable *field* to the second field of the input specification, sets the variable *type* to the first character of the third field of the input specification, and sets the variable *content* to the portion of the third field lying within the outermost parentheses.

The next three lines of the program print out the values of these variables as comments within the generated code to facilitate debugging.

The remainder of the main body of this portion of the generator is run *iff* this line of the specification is one which specifies the length of the field, i.e. if the first character of the third field of the specification is an *L*. In that case, *lolim* is set to the lower limit of

129

the range to be checked and *hilim* is set to the upper limit. Both limits are printed out as a comment, and the three lines following generate the code which actually checks the length of the field.

The complete output of the generator on the given specification is the following program:

EXAMPLE - A Data Validator

```
# field = 1
# type = R
# content = a
$1 !~ /a/ {
     print "line #" NR " field #1 - Must contain an 'a'"
     }
# field = 2
# type = S
# content = alpha,beta
# pat = ^alpha$|^beta$
$2 !~ /^alpha$|^beta$/ {
     print "line #" NR " field #2 - Must be alpha or beta"
     }
# field = 3
# type = L
# content = 4,7
# comma = 2
# lolim = 4; hilim = 7
length($3) < 4 || length($3) > 7{
     print "line #" NR " field #3 - Must have length between 4 and 7'
     }
# field = 4
# type = N
# content = 5,8
# comma = 2
```

```
# lolim = 5; hilim = 8
$4 !~ /[0-9][0-9]*/ || $4 < 5 || $4 > 8 {
print "line #" NR " field #4 - Must be integer between 5 and 8"
}
```

The output of the generated program when run against the
specification is the following set of error messages, since the
specification does not conform to the syntax that *it* is specifying:

```
line #1 field #1 - Must contain an 'a'
line #1 field #2 - Must be alpha or beta
line #1 field #4 - Must be integer between 5 and 8
line #2 field #1 - Must contain an 'a'
line #2 field #2 - Must be alpha or beta
line #2 field #3 - Must have length between 4 and 7
line #2 field #4 - Must be integer between 5 and 8
line #3 field #1 - Must contain an 'a'
line #3 field #2 - Must be alpha or beta
line #3 field #4 - Must be integer between 5 and 8
line #4 field #1 - Must contain an 'a'
line #4 field #2 - Must be alpha or beta
line #4 field #4 - Must be integer between 5 and 8
```

6.6 Significance of the Example

The validator presented in this chapter is a minimal example of
the method of metaprogramming. The validator is produced by code
generation techniques so that the code is uniform. Any changes to
the validator are made either in the specification used to generate

132

the code or in the program that translates the specification into a validation program. In the case of changes to the specification, the validator may be used to check the syntax of the specification and, furthermore, the repeated use and testing of the generating program gives us a high level of assurance that it is functioning properly. In the case of changes to the generating program, we can check that it is producing valid code which gives some assurance of its correctness.

Some of the characteristics of the example apply in general. The generator is specific to the application for which it is intended. It performs its intended function and no more, thereby avoiding the complexity that often makes software unmaintainable. The code for the example is fairly concise, and the specifications are easily understood. This simplicity gives us confidence that we can get the generator right the first time and it also makes the code maintainable.

The example is deceptive in its simplicity. More typical applications of metaprogramming are very computation intensive, relying on the computer to do all of the transformations that are necessary to develop a working program from a mathematical model described in a notation that is suitable for application specialists.

A complete application will require a collection of such specialized components, but each of them should be constructed using the metaprogramming technique: develop a simple specification language embodying a well-understood algorithmic method, and construct a program or set of programs to translate the specification into an executable program.

Chapter 7

Software Economics

Here we develop the basic economic theory of the metaprogramming method presented in Chapter 3. In the next chapter we present a computational model and a program based on this theory.

7.1 Introduction

Given a description of a programming project, how are the resources needed to satisfactorily complete it to be estimated? A cost model such as the one described in Section 3.3 could be used. This would estimate the development costs and schedule based on a model of smoothed historical data. But unless the model were adjusted for increases in programmer productivity, such an estimate would be overly conservative and might be unsuccessful in winning a programming contract. In either case, such an approach presumes that the production of programs is a slowly changing technology.

Furthermore, such an approach inhibits the redistribution of investment of time and effort in the various phases of the project. If the costs of any particular activity is assumed to be a fixed fraction of total costs, then increasing that fraction will be seen as an increase in the overall cost. This accounts for the well known *WISCA* [1] syndrome, which often leads to details being fixed before their consequences are understood.

On the other hand, if our view of programming is correct, then very substantial gains in programmer productivity are achievable by appropriate resource allocation. This requires that a significant fraction of any project be dedicated to enhancing productivity and the construction of tools.

In this chapter, I proceed on the assumption that ultra-high programmer productivity is achievable and explore some of the consequences. In fact, suitable techniques are available but they have been applied only to parts of programming projects. This has vitiated their overall effect.

Next is the problem of determining the fraction of project effort that should be devoted to productivity enhancement. In order to choose the right fraction I indicate what factors must be considered. These factors will probably vary from project to project, but the general method of determining the fraction is shown.

In the concluding parts of this chapter I discuss the elements of risk and competition. By investing heavily in productivity, there is the risk that project commitments may not be met. It is not much good for a customer who has ordered a compiler to be informed that the compiler is not ready but that a compiler-compiler [2] now exists. On the other hand, not using the best programming technology could lessen productivity. The developer is thus caught between the Scylla and Charybdis of being too radical or too conservative.

7.2 On Ultra-High Programmer Productivity [3]

> I have seen a small manufactory of this kind where ten men only were employed, and where some of them consequently performed two or three distinct operations. Those ten persons, therefore, could make among them upwards of forty-eight thousand pins in a day. But if they had all wrought separately and independently, and without any of them having been educated to this peculiar business, they certainly could not each of them have made twenty, perhaps not one pin in a day.
>
> Adam Smith, *The Wealth of Nations*

In our model of ultra-high programmer productivity (UHPP) we assume that some methodology for producing software very economically exists, but that the methodology is only applicable to

---

[1] *Why Isn't Sam Coding Anything?*

[2] A compiler-compiler is a software tool, i.e. program, to assist in constructing compilers.

[3] This section expands and generalizes [Levy 1982].

138

some fraction (possibly, almost all) of the project. Under those assumptions:

1. The overall productivity will approach asymptotically to a limit determined by the fraction of the software that uses normal software development techniques.

2. The benefit to be derived from extending the domain of applicability of UHPP techniques is much greater than the benefit to be derived from increasing the effectiveness of those techniques [4].

3. The increase of productivity resulting from applying two UHPP techniques to independent portions of the software is more than the product of the increases in productivity of the techniques applied separately.

The conclusion to be drawn from this relatively simple model is that a methodology offering 100% applicability of UHPP techniques is most desirable.

---

[4] The analysis given in this section is incomplete in that the costs of these two options are not assessed, but we believe that including these costs in the analysis would only strengthen the conclusions.

7.3 Economic Fundamentals

In the so-called classical theory of the firm, we analyze a production function, y, as a function of factors of production, x_i. In

$$y = f(x_1, x_2)$$

where the product price is π, and factor costs p_1 and p_2, the net

$$R = \pi y - (p_1 x_1 + p_2 x_2)$$

The necessary condition for maximizing revenue is

$$\frac{\partial R}{\partial x_1} = \frac{\partial R}{\partial x_2} = 0$$

so that

$$\pi \frac{\partial f}{\partial x_1} - p_1 = \pi \frac{\partial f}{\partial x_2} - p_2 = 0$$

leading to the relationship

$$\frac{p_1}{\frac{\partial f}{\partial x_1}} = \frac{p_2}{\frac{\partial f}{\partial x_2}} == \pi$$

In words, the relative usage of the factors of production should be such that the marginal rate of substitution between them (i.e. the ratio of marginal products $\frac{\partial f}{\partial x_1} \Big/ \frac{\partial f}{\partial x_2}$, is equal to the the given price ratio, [Allen]).

Furthermore, if only one of the factors of production is variable in the short run, we can analyze the expansion of production by applying more of that particular function. The production function, $y = f(x)$, will, in general, exhibit diminishing returns to scale after some point, and ultimately the marginal cost of that factor of production will exceed the marginal revenue obtained from it.

In the case of software development, we modify this approach by considering only one factor of production - the programming labor. One may utilize this labor in one of two ways:

- Develop programming tools - programs which make subsequent programming more efficient thereby raising productivity.

- Develop the software product directly.

In the first case, there is no immediate deliverable software produced but subsequent productivity is sufficiently enhanced to more than offset the investment in the tools. At each stage of the development of a software product we can, therefore, analyze what the marginal product of developing software tools is, and compare that marginal product to the marginal product of directly developing the deliverable software. The marginal product of deliverable software may be taken to be just the number of lines of code produced. The marginal product of developing software tools is the effort that is subsequently saved in producing the deliverable software.

In this section I formulate a mathematical model of this tradeoff. In Chapter 8, I discuss a computer program that performs this analysis for a project based on given parameters.

7.3.1 Motivation for the Mathematical Model In this model, I explain why software development has not fully exploited some of the state-of-the-art productivity techniques to increase programmer output and reduce costs [5]. I formulate a model of software productivity as an initial approximation; the model shows that in averaging high productivity techniques and low productivity techniques the effect of high productivity techniques is diluted. This answer is convincing, as far as it goes, but is incomplete as a guide for decision-making in any specific case.

7.3.2 The Problem Software productivity is the subject of serious concern to computer users. Several techniques for achieving ultra-high productivity increases in software development have been identified, where ultra-high productivity gains are defined as productivity gains $>> 5$. Why have these techniques not allayed the concerns about lagging software productivity?

7.3.3 The Model A simple model which provides a solution to the problem stated above is the following: We assume that an ultra-highly productive software methodology, m, is used which is

---

[5] For cases demonstrating the extremely high productivity gains possible see [Levinson], [Levy 1985], or [Bassett].

applicable to a fraction, k, of the software to be developed, and that, where the method is applicable, it reduces the software cost by a factor, g. The rest of the software, $1 - k$, is developed as usual.

Γ, the overall productivity gain is defined as

$$\Gamma = \frac{E_0}{E_m}$$

where E_0 is the effort required to produce software without m, and E_m is the effort required to produce software using m.

Since we are interested only in the ratio $\dfrac{E_0}{E_m}$ we can normalize and set $E_0 = 1$. Then

$$E_m = \frac{k}{g} + 1 - k. \tag{1}$$

In our model Γ is a function of k and g and thus

$$\Gamma[k,g] = \frac{1}{\dfrac{k}{g}+1-k} = \frac{g}{k+(1-k)g} \tag{2}$$

Two cases are of immediate interest:

$$\lim_{k \to 1} \Gamma \to g \tag{3a}$$

so that as m becomes applicable to all the software the value of Γ is asymptotic to g, and

$$\lim_{g \to \infty} \Gamma \to \frac{1}{1-k} \tag{3b}$$

so that as g becomes unbounded, Γ approaches a constant.

Very high productivities, g, applied even to large portions of the software can be seen from Equation 3b to have apparently moderate effects on overall productivity, Γ. For example, $k = \frac{2}{3}$ and $g = \infty$, which is the case of using unlimited productivity gains on $\frac{2}{3}$ of the software, increases overall productivity by a factor of only 3.

7.3.4 Model Dynamics Next let us consider changes in overall productivity arising from changes in k and g.

$$d\Gamma = \frac{\partial \Gamma}{\partial k} dk + \frac{\partial \Gamma}{\partial g} dg \tag{4}$$

Using Equation 2 and simplifying:

$$\frac{\partial \Gamma}{\partial g} = \frac{k}{g^2} \cdot \Gamma^2 \tag{4a}$$

$$\frac{\partial \Gamma}{\partial k} = \left[1 - \frac{1}{g} \right] \Gamma^2 \tag{4b}$$

The ratio of Equations 4a and 4b is

144

$$\frac{\dfrac{\partial \Gamma}{\partial k}}{\dfrac{\partial \Gamma}{\partial g}} = \frac{g^2\left[1-\dfrac{1}{g}\right]}{k} \tag{4c}$$

Therefore, the effect of changes in k, the domain of applicability of the ultra-high productivity techniques is much greater than the effect of changes in g. Equation 4c says that much more benefit is to be derived from extending the domain of applicability of ultra-high productivity techniques than from increasing the productivity gains of those techniques.

7.3.4.1 The Effect of Doubling g Let $\Gamma_{-,n}$ denote the increase of productivity obtained from increasing g by a factor of n while holding k constant.

$$\Gamma_{-,2} = \frac{\Gamma[k,2g]}{\Gamma[k,g]} = \frac{1-k+\dfrac{k}{g}}{1-k+\dfrac{k}{2g}} \tag{5}$$

$$\approx 1 + \frac{k}{2(1-k)g} + o\left(\frac{k}{g^2}\right) \tag{5'}$$

Therefore, doubling g has a comparatively small effect on productivity. For example,

$$\Gamma_{-,2}\left[\frac{2}{3},10\right] = 1.091$$

7.3.4.2 Effect of Reducing 1 - k by a Factor of 2 Let $r = 1 - k$. Then

$$\Gamma[r,g] = \frac{1}{\frac{1-r}{g} + r}$$

and let $\Gamma_{m,-}$ denote the change in productivity obtained from reducing r by a factor of $\frac{1}{m}$ while holding g constant.

$$\Gamma_{.5,-} = \frac{\frac{1-r}{g} + r}{\frac{1-\frac{r}{2}}{g} + \frac{r}{2}} \tag{6}$$

$$\approx 2\left[1 - \frac{1}{r(g-1)}\right] \tag{6'}$$

Using the same 'operating point' as in Section 7.3.4.1, we have

$$\Gamma_{.5,-}\left[\frac{2}{3}, 10\right] = 1.6$$

7.3.5 Effect of Two Productivity Methods - Synergy This section demonstrates that the gains from applying two different productivity techniques m_1 and m_2 is greater than would be realized by taking the product of the gains due to m_1 and m_2 taken separately. The assumption is that the two productivity enhancement techniques have non-overlapping domains of applicability and are applicable to different components of the software.

Let m_1 and m_2 be two different productivity methods, with productivity gains g_1 and g_2, respectively, and domains of applicability k_1 and k_2.

Let $\Gamma_{1,2}$ be the productivity gain due to the joint application of m_1 and m_2.

Example To clarify the meaning of the variables k_i, g_i, and Γ_i, consider a project where a productivity gain of 2 due to a method m_1 applies to 40% of the project, and a productivity gain of 5 due to a method m_2 applies to a different 25% of the project. Then $k_1 = .4$, $g_1 = 2$, $k_2 = .25$, and $g_2 = 10$.

The effect of a factor of two (2) gain in productivity applied to 40% of a project is to speed up the total project by

$$\Gamma_1 = \frac{1}{1 - .4 + \dfrac{.4}{2}} = \frac{1}{.8} = 1.25$$

The effect of a factor of ten (10) gain in productivity applied to 25% of a project is to speed up the total project by

$$\Gamma_2 = \frac{1}{1 - .25 + \dfrac{.25}{10}} = \frac{1}{.775} = 1.29$$

Thus, each Γ_i measures the *overall project productivity gain* that

147

would be achieved by a gain g_i applied to a fraction k_i of the project, *assuming that no productivity gains are achieved in other parts of the project.*

$$\Gamma_{1,2} = \cfrac{1}{\cfrac{k_1}{g_1} + \cfrac{k_2}{g_2} + 1 - k_1 - k_2} \tag{7}$$

$$\Gamma_1 \cdot \Gamma_2 = \cfrac{1}{\left(\cfrac{k_1}{g_1} + 1 - k_1\right)} \cdot \cfrac{1}{\left(\cfrac{k_2}{g_2} + 1 - k_2\right)} \tag{8}$$

$$= \cfrac{1}{\left(\cfrac{k_1}{g_1} + \cfrac{k_2}{g_2} + 1 - k_1 - k_2\right) + k_1\left(1 - \cfrac{1}{g_1}\right) \cdot k_2\left(1 - \cfrac{1}{g_2}\right)}$$

$$= \cfrac{1}{\alpha + k_1\left(1 - \cfrac{1}{g_1}\right) \cdot k_2\left(1 - \cfrac{1}{g_2}\right)}$$

where $\alpha = \dfrac{1}{\Gamma_{1,2}}$. Now

$$\Gamma_i = \cfrac{1}{1 - k_i\left(1 - \cfrac{1}{g_i}\right)}$$

so

148

Economic Fundamentals

$$k_i\left(1-\frac{1}{g_i}\right)=1-\frac{1}{\Gamma_i} \tag{9}$$

Substitute Equation 9 into Equation 8 and using Equation 7

$$\Gamma_1\cdot\Gamma_2 = \frac{1}{\dfrac{1}{\Gamma_{1,2}}+\left(1-\dfrac{1}{\Gamma_1}\right)\cdot\left(1-\dfrac{1}{\Gamma_2}\right)} \tag{10}$$

which can be rearranged as [6]

$$\Gamma_{1,2} = \Gamma_1\cdot\Gamma_2\left(\frac{1}{1-(\Gamma_1-1)\cdot(\Gamma_2-1)}\right) \tag{10'}$$

If both methods m_1 and m_2 are applied, the total productivity gain, $\Gamma_{1,2}$, given by Equation 7 is

$$\Gamma_{1,2} = \frac{1}{1-(.4+.25)+\dfrac{.4}{2}+\dfrac{.25}{10}} = \frac{1}{1-.65+.225} = \frac{1}{.575} = 1.74$$

Now

$$\Gamma_{1,2} = 1.74 > \Gamma_1\cdot\Gamma_2 = 1.25\times1.29 = 1.61$$

---

[6] The factor in the denominator $(\Gamma_1-1)\cdot(\Gamma_2-1)$ can be shown to be less than one under the assumption that $k_1 + k_2 < 1$

The synergy effect, as given by Equation 10' is

$$\frac{1}{1 - (\Gamma_1 - 1)\cdot(\Gamma_2 - 1)} = \frac{1}{1 - .25 \times .29} = \frac{1}{1 - .0725} = \frac{1}{.9275} = 1.078$$

and $1.078 \times 1.61 = 1.74$. Thus

$$\Gamma_1 \cdot \Gamma_2 \times \textit{the synergy factor} = \Gamma_{1,2}$$

7.3.5.1 Generalized Synergy Theorem [7] We can generalize Equation 10 as follows: Let

$$\Gamma_i = \frac{1}{\dfrac{k_i}{g_i} + 1 - k_i}$$

Then

$$\Gamma_{1,2,\dots,n} = \frac{1}{\displaystyle\sum_{i=1}^{n} \left(\frac{k_i}{g_i}\right) + 1 - \sum_{i=1}^{n} k_i}$$

where $\Gamma_{1,2,\dots,n}$ is the productivity gain from jointly applying factors $m_1, m_2, \dots, m_n$.

Let

$$\Pi_n = (\Gamma_{i_1} - 1)\cdot(\Gamma_{i_2} - 1)\cdots(\Gamma_{i_n} - 1) \qquad i_1 < i_2 < \dots < i_n$$

---

[7] I am indebted to Professor Michael Lin of the Department of Mathematics and Computer Science of Ben Gurion University for the initial proof of this theorem. The proof given here is my own.

and let

$$\sigma_n^N = \Sigma \Pi_n$$

taken over all possible choices of indices of Π_n, where the i_j range from 1 to N. Then the general theorem relating the composite overall gain, $\Gamma_{1,2,\ldots,n}$, to the individual gains, Γ_i, is

$$\Gamma_{1,2,\ldots,n} = \frac{\Gamma_1 \cdot \Gamma_2 \cdots \Gamma_n}{1 - \sum_{j=2}^{n}(j-1)\sigma_j^n} \quad \triangleq \quad \phi_n$$

Proof: Let

$$\Gamma_i = \frac{1}{\dfrac{k_i}{g_i} - k_i + 1} = \frac{1}{1 - s_i}$$

Then

$$s_i = k_i - \frac{k_i}{g_i} = 1 - \frac{1}{\Gamma_i}$$

$$\phi_n = \frac{1}{1 - \sum_{i=1}^{n} s_i}$$

$$\frac{1}{\phi_n} = 1 - \sum_{i=1}^{n} s_i = \frac{1}{\phi_{n-1}} - s_n = \frac{1}{\phi_{n-1}} + 1 - \frac{1}{\Gamma_n} = 1 - \sum_{i=1}^{n}\left(1 - \frac{1}{\Gamma_i}\right)$$

$$\rho_n = \frac{\Gamma_1 \cdot \Gamma_2 \cdots \Gamma_n}{\Gamma_{1,2,\ldots,n}} = (1-n) \cdot \prod_{i=1}^{n} \Gamma_i + \sum_{i=1}^{n} \prod_{j \neq i} \Gamma_j$$

$$\frac{d}{d\Gamma_1} \cdot \frac{d}{d\Gamma_1} \cdots \frac{d}{d\Gamma_n} \rho_n = (1-n)$$

so that ρ_n is multinomial in $\Gamma_i - 1$. Now I show by induction that

$$\rho_n = 1 - \sum_{j=2}^{n}(j-1)\sigma_j^n$$

Thus the induction must show that given the preceding equation

$$\rho_{n+1} = 1 - \sum_{j=2}^{n} (j-1)\sigma_j^{n+1} - n\sigma_n^{n+1}$$

$$= 1 - \sum_{j=2}^{n} (j-1)\sigma_j^{n+1} - n \cdot \prod_{i=1}^{n+1} (\Gamma_i - 1)$$

The $\sum(j-1)\sigma_j$ term follows by symmetry and reduction to the case of ρ_n when any Γ_j is 1. The $\Pi(\Gamma_i - 1)$ term follows from the observation about the derivative.

7.3.6 Interpretation What does all of this imply about the application of ultra-high productivity techniques in programming? It appears that once a high productivity technique is available to deal with one part of the application, it is more important to develop high productivity techniques for those portions not yet covered than it is to perfect the available techniques. Furthermore, the importance of obtaining coverage for the remaining segments of the program becomes more significant as that uncovered fraction decreases. This suggests that techniques that afford 100% coverage, should be especially attractive. The only techniques that seem to offer promise for 100% coverage are those which depend on a formal specification from which *all* of the code can be generated. *Unfortunately, this seems to be beyond the current state of the art.*

Next consider the synergistic effect of different techniques. Since the productivity gains of two techniques applied jointly is greater than the product of the productivity gains of these techniques applied separately, and since no single technique appears able to provide 100% coverage a number of different methods should be developed independently. This provides a rationale for specialization. Perhaps when software is developed by specialists, each concentrating on one aspect of the development where they can be held accountable for the productivity of that aspect, we may be able to achieve gains comparable to those noted by Adam Smith.

7.3.7 Speculations and Open Questions I started by asking the question: Why have ultra-high productivity techniques not been more widely applied? My simple answer is that *very high productivity techniques get swamped by normal productivities.* The practical effect of this is that managers of software development looking at *overall* productivities conclude that ultra-high productivity techniques are at best an evolutionary technique with modest benefits to the development.

My own speculation is that virtually all software can be produced using ultra-high productivity techniques, although that is not proved here. What I do show is that the greatest returns are to be realized from increasing the productivities of those areas that have marginal productivities. But the bottom line is return on investment: How much does it cost to get the returns? In the rest of this chapter I address this issue.

My experience is that the ultra-high productivity techniques are so effective that the cost of tool development is amortized extremely quickly - even in a one year development project. I speculate that much greater returns on investment are available. *The rationale for this assertion is that I do not believe that the cost of applying ultra-high productivity techniques to the marginal components will be any higher than the initial cost of applying those methods.* Indeed the costs should go down because the first application of ultra-high productivity techniques requires developing components that make the rest of the job easier. (Example: Initially one has to build data dictionaries and supporting routines. These dictionaries and routines can be used throughout.) Further, the productivity gains increase significantly as coverage increases.

Certainly the use of ultra-high productivity techniques entails a higher risk since innovation is needed. And innovation requires changes and encounters inertia and insecurity. These effects are known and are qualitative factors that have reduced the impact of ultra-high productivity techniques.

If the case for ultra-high productivity techniques can be made convincingly and quantitatively, managers will be able to gain confidence in their use. This book is a small step along the way.

154

7.4 Investing in the Project

We assume that during the development a total of n units is to be expended by the project. Of these n units, n_1 are to be initially invested in software tools and techniques for increasing productivity. The remaining $n - n_1$ units will then be used to 'produce' the object code to be delivered. Let $f(n_1)$ be the rate of production of object code. Then $f(n_1)$ can be expected to be a monotonic increasing function of n_1, since additional investment in productivity tools should never decrease the productivity.

We can determine n_1 which will maximize the total output of object code for a given fixed project budget, n. The total object code, C, is given by:

$$C = (n - n_1)f(n_1) \tag{11}$$
$$= nf(n_1) - n_1 f(n_1) \tag{11a}$$

To maximize C, differentiate C with respect to n_1 and set the derivative equal to 0.

$$\frac{dC}{dn_1} = \frac{d}{dn_1}[nf(n_1) - n_1 f(n_1)]$$

and, denoting $\frac{df}{dn_1}$ by $f'(n_1)$, we have

$$n - n_1 = \frac{f(n_1)}{f'(n_1)} \tag{13}$$

$$n_1 = n - \frac{f(n_1)}{f'(n_1)} \tag{13a}$$

$$\frac{n_1}{n} = 1 - \frac{f(n_1)}{nf'(n_1)} \tag{14}$$

7.4.1 Linear Growth of $f(n)$

A linear growth in productivity can be represented by the equation:

$$f(n_1) = f_0 + kn_1 \tag{15}$$

In Equation 15, f_0 is lines-of-code/staff-year, n is staff-years, and k is lines-of-code/staff-year/year. If the number of staff-years of effort, N, needed to produce the tools and techniques to double productivity is known, then Equation 15 can be rewritten as

$$2f_0 = f_0 + kN \tag{16}$$

and the constant, k, is then determined by

$$k = \frac{f_0}{N}$$

The constant $\dfrac{f_0}{k}$ is also important and is equal to the staff-years needed to double productivity (in the linear growth model). Maximum output is obtained by choosing

$$n_1 = \max(0, \frac{n}{2} - \frac{f_0}{2k}) \tag{17}$$

When $n_1 > 0$, we have

$$\frac{n_1}{n} = \frac{1}{2} - \frac{f_0}{2kn} \tag{18}$$

In this case somewhat less than 50% of project resources should be expended to increase productivity to maximize total project output. (Note that in the limit when n is large the ratio to be spent on increasing productivity should approach 50% - *independent of k*.)

7.4.2 Quadratic Growth of *f(n)*

A quadratic growth in productivity is one determined by the equation:

$$f(n_1) = f_0 + kn_1^2 \qquad (19)$$

Maximum output is obtained by choosing

$$n_1 = \frac{2n}{3} - \frac{f_0}{3kn_1} \qquad (20)$$

Now as n becomes large, n_1 approaches $\frac{2n}{3}$, - *again, independent of k*.

7.4.3 Exponential Growth of *f(n)*

An exponential growth in productivity is one determined by the equation:

$$f(n_1) = f_0 e^{rn_1} \qquad (21)$$

Differentiating Equation 21, we have

$$\frac{df(n_1)}{n_1} = f_0 re^{rn_1} = rf(n_1) \qquad (22)$$

Using the basic equation for maximizing output we have

$$n_1 = n - \frac{1}{r} \qquad (23)$$

$1/r$ when the actual software product is generated.

7.5 Risk

In the discussion of investing, the assumption was that the project activity would be divided into two phases:

1. a tool and productivity development phase

2. a 'production' phase.

This simplification of the development process is useful for determining what fraction of the total project effort should be 'invested'.

If the total project consists of a development followed by a production phase, and if the production phase is made very short, then there is a significant chance that the tools will not accomplish their purpose. Clearly, the production phase must be followed by some testing, but if sufficient time has not been allowed for needed fixes to the tools, then project commitments may not be met. Also the more time and effort that is spent developing tools, the greater the quantity of code that they will contain, and the less chance there will be for making the tools error-free.

We have discussed elsewhere [8] how the use of suitable code

Risk

generation techniques can lead to software which is of higher quality and uniformity than hand-written code. The reason for this is that the code generators are effectively tested may times during their development, and those tests also serve as tests of the final products. Still, a failure of the software tools could result in no end product.

An analogy may help to clarify this point. If, on the one hand, you produce automobiles, then at the end of the production cycle you have a small number of vehicles. On the other hand, if you construct automated factories with all the associated tooling, a failure late in the development cycle is much more critical since you may not be able to produce *any* automobiles. It is an all or nothing situation.

It would be desirable to have some quantitative measures of this risk as an aid to decision making [9]. This would allow one to

---

[8] [Levinson], summarized in Chapter 3.
[9] I realize the role of intuition in making such decisions, but believe that it is strengthened when there are quantitative techniques to test and refine it. Even when one has decided to use such an approach, it is not clear what specific measures should be taken. [Carlson] has written:

"Three examples of paradigms of decision making illustrate the variety of decision-making processes. The first example is the rational (economic) paradigm, which postulates that decision processes attempt to maximize the expected value of a decision by determining payoffs, costs, and risks for alternatives. A second paradigm asserts that the decision-making process is compare the probable effects of of alternative courses of action and could be used as a basis for evaluation.

Let us define a probability distribution, $R(t)$, which denotes the probability that the project is completed satisfactorily by time t. We may then assume the following:

$$R(t) = 0 \quad \text{for } t < t_0 \tag{24a}$$

where t_0 is the earliest possible completion date for the project, and

$$R(t) = 1 \quad \textit{as t becomes large} \tag{24b}$$

and $R(t)$ is monotonically increasing. In comparing two approaches to software development we may denote the risk of project i, R_i and the earliest possible completion date t_i. If the form of $R_i(t)$ is known for the two approaches and t_i is known for one of the approaches, then it is possible to determine what value of t_i should be chosen for the other project to achieve the same level of risk at any specified point of time.

---

one of finding the first cost-effective alternative by using simple heuristics rather than optimal search techniques. A third paradigm describes decision-making as a process of successive limited comparisons in order to reach a consensus on one alternative."

EXAMPLE: A reasonable guess for *R(t)* is

$$R_i(t) = 1 - e^{k_i(t - t_i)} \qquad (25)$$

Then we may say that the more risky project has a smaller value of k_i so that its probability of completion approaches 1 more slowly. Now using Equation 25, a given value of k_i and t_i, and a given level of risk we can determine *t*. Then using Equation 25 and the other k_i we can determine the value of the corresponding t_i which will give the same risk at the same instant of time.

Using this analysis, the riskier the method chosen to develop a program, the earlier must be its scheduled completion date. This is because its risk distribution converges more slowly. So it is possible, in theory, to compensate for a riskier approach by alternative scheduling. A possible advantage of this is that in the more risky approach there is a possibility of finishing ahead of the earliest possible date of the more conservative approach. On the other hand, since the risky approach has a larger variance, the scheduled completion date may also be missed by a larger amount.

It would also seem that k_i in Equation 25 should depend on both the overall project size, *O*, and the manner in which the project is organized. Intuitively, *k* should increase with *O* perhaps as the square root of *O*.

Furthermore, if the project development plan is organized as an acyclic directed ordered graph [10] one might derive a more 'normal' distribution for the overall project, assuming that each edge in the graph has an independent distribution of the form of Equation 25.

While accounting for the element of risk, it is necessary to realize the salubrious effects of presenting a technical team with a challenge [11]. Intangible factors, such as project morale, are often the critical factors in the success or failure of a project. As [Brooks] has written:

> A baseball manager recognizes a nonphysical talent, *hustle*, as an essential gift of great players and great teams. It is the characteristic of running faster than necessary, moving sooner than necessary, trying harder than necessary. It is essential for great programming teams, too. Hustle provides the cushion, the reserve capacity, that enables a team to cope with routine mishaps, to anticipate and forfend minor calamities.

---

[10] PERT charts are such a project plan.
[11] See, e.g. [Kidder].

7.6 Competition

In the absence of competition, a software entrepreneur could be expected to determine the cost of programming in accordance with the model of software costs given in Section 3.3, or with any of the other familiar software costing models. Purchasers would then expect to pay this as the fair market price for the software. Having determined the selling price, the vendor is then free to reorganize his software production to minimize development costs at some acceptable level of risk.

In a competitive situation, a vendor could determine the price of the software at each level of risk. Determining the optimum method of producing the software would proceed as follows:

1. Obtain an estimate of the size of the program to be produced.

2. Using one of the investment models of Section 7.4, determine the values of n and n_1. For example, using the exponential model of Section 7.4.3, we have from Equations 21 and 22:

    $$L = \frac{1}{r} f_0 e^{rn - 1} \tag{26}$$

    where L is the number of lines of code to be produced. This allows you to determine n and then, using Equation 23, n_1.

3. Having determined n, we can determine t_0 which is the earliest date for project completion.

163

4. Knowing t_0, and using the methods of Section 7.5, we can determine t_1 the actual delivery date for a suitable level of risk.

Using the above method, you assume that the price of the software to be delivered to the customer is fixed by the price of programming - and other support activities - at the current rate of productivity, but that the software is actually produced using UHPP techniques at a substantially lower cost. This method would lead to economic profits inducing other entrepreneurs to enter the software market, driving the price of software down to its economic cost. Standard economic theory can then be used, knowing the price of the commodity and the market situation, to determine the point of maximum profitability for the firm.

7.7 A Complete Example

Consider a hypothetical project requiring 36,000 lines of programming where the nominal rate of programming is 3,000 lines per staff-year at the current state-of-the-art. One would expect to have to pay for 12 staff-years of programming (appropriately burdened). Using the methodology of Section 7.4, consider how this cost can be reduced.

First let us consider the exponential growth model. Assume that $r = \frac{1}{3}$; in other words, 3 staff-years are sufficient to build the tools and techniques to double subsequent programming productivity. Use Equation 21,

$$36,000 = 3 * 3,000(e^{\frac{n}{3}} - 1)$$

to determine n, which yields $n = 7.16$. Thus 7.16 staff-years of programming are required to do the job rather than the nominal 12.

If we assume that the project duration is proportional to the logarithm of the effort required, then the minimal project duration using the methodology of Section 7.4 should be about 78% of the minimal project duration using state-of-the-art programming rates. If the nominal project effort was 12 staff years, at an average staffing level of 4 people, then the project would require 3 years to complete. With the simple risk model of Equation 25 doubling the risk doubles the time to achieve a given confidence level. In other words, if a 90% confidence level of completion of the project can be achieved within one year of the earliest possible delivery date in the nominal case, then using an approach which is twice as risky would require a two year buffer to achieve the same confidence level.

In our example then, with these assumptions, the nominal development approach would take 12 staff-years, three years to earliest delivery, and one more year to be 90% confident of delivery. Using a software tools and techniques approach requires 7.16 staff-years, an earliest completion date of 2.34 years, and two more years to be 90% confident of delivery.

A similar analysis is possible for other growth models. For example, in the linear growth model

$$O = (n - n_1)(f_0 + kn_1)$$

Substituting $\dfrac{n}{2} - \dfrac{f_0}{2k}$ for n, and simplifying, we have

$$O = \frac{k}{4} * (\frac{f_0}{k} + n)^2$$

or $n = \sqrt{(\dfrac{4O}{k})} - \dfrac{f_0}{k}.$

The values of $\dfrac{f_0}{k}$ and k comparable to the exponential analysis are 3 and 1,000, respectively. Hence, the total project effort is $n=9$ staff-years of which 3 staff-years are spent doubling productivity from 3,000 lines-of-code/staff-year to 6,000 lines-of-code/staff-year and then the 'product' is generated in 6 staff years.

All that is claimed for these numbers is the general phenomenon that they exhibit. Namely, investing in the tools and techniques of program productivity using the metaprogramming method as analyzed in Section 7.4 has a significant impact on productivity.

Chapter 8

The Model

Chapter 7 develops the economic theory of the metaprogramming method. The metaphor for the method is a factory production line with the initial phases of the software development concentrating on setting up the assembly line.

While analysis of the model for very simple cases can be performed analytically, as has been done in Chapter 7, more detailed studies will need computer modelling. In this chapter, I present a relatively simple computer model which contains the essence of what more complicated models would need. The model simulates the development process, and calculates the returns in programmer productivity of initial resource investment in the software models and tools.

The Model

A computer program was written based on the analysis of Chapter 7, to allow more detailed study of the effects of different decisions in the software development cycle on the overall cost of product development. The program models the major factors in software development and is sufficiently general in its overall approach to allow adaptation for detailed studies where more specific information on costs and staff schedules is available.

The program "runs" a development project on a month by month basis.

Assume, in accordance with the analysis given in Chapter 7, that the early stages of the project are devoted to the development of tools and productivity enhancement. Then each month a determination is made whether to continue software tool development or whether to change to the programming of the deliverable software product. This decision can be made in one of four ways:

1. *Fixed percent of estimated effort* - Estimate at the project outset how much programming effort, in staff months, would be required to complete the project. Some fixed percentage of this effort is then allocated as the preliminary development effort.

2. *Fixed estimated time* - Estimate at the project outset what the total project duration should be. The initial phase of the

project is constrained to meet this objective.

3. *Fixed estimated effort* - Estimate at the project outset what the total project effort should be. The initial phase of the project is constrained to meet this objective.

4. *Marginal cost / marginal revenue* - At the start of each month estimate what the savings in programming costs for the remainder of the project will be based on the projected increases in productivity that can be achieved over the next month. As long as the projected savings exceeds the cost of the additional preliminary development effort, continue to work on software tool development. As soon as the projected costs exceed the anticipated savings, stop the preliminary tool development and proceed to work on the deliverable software directly.

In the prototype program presented later in this chapter, the decision criterion is contained in one subroutine where the decision is made whether or not to continue the production enhancement phase. Therefore, it is quite easy to add other criteria to the model.

While it seems clear from an economic point of view that the marginal analysis is the most sound from a theoretical point of view, experience indicates that managers are often more comfortable with fixed percentage guidelines.

After the switch from the initial development phase to the production phase, the program continues to model the production phase on a monthly basis until the required software has been produced.

Once the program has run the project to completion, the summary statistics are developed and compared to the standard COCOMO model where the user can select the project type of the COCOMO model.

It should be reemphasized that the model and the program are intentionally designed to have the flavor of *back of the envelope* calculations. The model is intended to highlight the effects of the revised development methodology. More refined models can be developed and the parameters of the model tuned to a particular organization's experience.

8.1 Parameters of the Model

The model requires the user to provide the following parameters:

Program size   The user specifies the size of the program being produced in thousands of source instruction lines, KDSI. KDSI is chosen because of the lack of anything that is a demonstrably better predictor of cost.

170

Initial staff size

The model as programmed assumes a simple exponential growth rate of the staff. The user specifies the initial staff size and the number of months required to double the staff. Since the staff growth model is a separate subprogram, it would not be difficult to add more sophisticated staffing schedules, e.g. a Rayleigh distribution based growth pattern.

In a more complete program incorporating this basic model, it should be possible for the user to leave the initial staff size unspecified and to have the program make a determination of the best size staff to start with. For preliminary studies, the user can try some different values and converge on the best one.

Staff time constant

The staff time constant is the number of months to double the staff size assuming a constant percentage growth rate.

171

The Model

Interest rate

A constant annual interest rate is assumed and the usual calculation of investment is carried forward. Again, more sophisticated economic modules can be used to account for inflation or deflation.

Productivity parameters

A set of parameters are used to estimate the growth of productivity, $P(t)$, where $P(t)$ is the number of lines of code that would be produced per month at time t. The model assumes that

$$P(t + 1) = f(n)*[a + b*t + c*P(t)] \, P(t)$$

where $f(n)$ is a factor that accounts for the size of the programming staff and the communication loss, discussed below.

Communication loss

It is generally agreed that as the number of programmers on a project is increased, there is a *decreasing return to scale* because programmers must take time to inform themselves about the work of other programmers. This is certainly one area where good management and suitable division of

172

labor can have very pronounced salubrious effects. We model the communication losses by assuming that $\frac{f(n)}{n}$ is monotonically decreasing of the form

$$f(n) = \frac{n}{1 + k*log(n)}$$

since intuitively the communication losses should be proportional to the logarithm of the number of programmers. Again, the communication loss factor is calculated in a separate subprogram which would allow one to substitute other models for this factor. The communication loss factor supplied by the user is the parameter k in the equation.

Decision criterion

Four possible criteria are used to switch between the productivity enhancement phase and the product development phase. The four choices in the prototype program are described in the preceding section. They are:

        o optimal from an economic point of view

        p fixed percent of estimated resources used for programming

        t fixed time for project completion

        s fixed total staff months for project completion.

Decision parameter   Three of the four decision criteria require the user to specify an additional parameter. If a fixed percentage of estimated resources is to be expended on productivity enhancement then the user must specify the percentage. If a fixed time is allocated to complete the project, the user must specify the time. If a fixed number of staff months is allowed, the user must specify the number of staff months.

8.2 A Sample Run

This section contains the output of the prototype modeling program. The program itself, written in Turbo Pascal, is given in the next section.

A Sample Run

A list of the input parameter values:

KDSI = 50.00
initial staff = 5.00
Cocomo type is **Embedded**
nominal rate = 200.00
a = 0.000; b = 0.000; c = 0.050
staff time constant = 40.00
communication loss factor = 0.50
annual interest rate = 18.00%
Decision criterion is **Optimal**

Productivity Enhancement Phase

Month = 1
Staff size = 5.00
Code rate = 200.00
Cumulative effort = 5.00
Investment = 5.00

Month = 2
Staff size = 5.09
Code rate = 228.05
Cumulative effort = 10.09
Investment = 10.16

Month = 3
Staff size = 5.18
Code rate = 260.45
Cumulative effort = 15.26
Investment = 15.49

Month = 4
Staff size = 5.27
Code rate = 297.91
Cumulative effort = 20.53
Investment = 20.99

A Sample Run

Month = 5
Staff size = 5.36
Code rate = 341.31
Cumulative effort = 25.89
Investment = 26.66

Month = 6
Staff size = 5.45
Code rate = 391.66
Cumulative effort = 31.34
Investment = 32.52

Month = 7
Staff size = 5.55
Code rate = 450.18
Cumulative effort = 36.89
Investment = 38.55

Month = 8
Staff size = 5.64
Code rate = 518.29
Cumulative effort = 42.53
Investment = 44.78

Month = 9
Staff size = 5.74
Code rate = 597.71
Cumulative effort = 48.28
Investment = 51.19

Month = 10
Staff size = 5.84
Code rate = 690.48
Cumulative effort = 54.12
Investment = 57.80

A Sample Run

Month = 11
Staff size =   5.95
Code rate =   799.01
Cumulative effort =   60.07
Investment =   64.62

Month = 12
Staff size =   6.05
Code rate =   926.22
Cumulative effort =   66.12
Investment =   71.63

Month = 13
Staff size =   6.16
Code rate = 1075.58
Cumulative effort =   72.27
Investment =   78.86

Month = 14
Staff size =　6.26
Code rate = 1251.26
Cumulative effort =　78.54
Investment =　86.31

Month = 15
Staff size =　6.37
Code rate = 1458.27
Cumulative effort =　84.91
Investment =　93.98

Month = 16
Staff size =　6.48
Code rate = 1702.64
Cumulative effort =　91.39
Investment =　101.87

A Sample Run

Month = 17
Staff size =   6.60
Code rate = 1991.66
Cumulative effort =   97.99
Investment =   110.00

Switch to Production Phase

Month = 18
Staff size =   6.71
Code rate = 2334.11
Code remaining = 41973.11
Cumulative effort =   104.70
Investment =   118.36

Month = 19
Staff size =   6.83
Code rate = 2334.11
Code remaining = 33842.01
Cumulative effort = 111.53
Investment = 126.97

Month = 20
Staff size =   6.95
Code rate = 2334.11
Code remaining = 25605.17
Cumulative effort = 118.48
Investment = 135.82

Month = 21
Staff size =   7.07
Code rate = 2334.11
Code remaining = 17261.07
Cumulative effort = 125.56
Investment = 144.93

A Sample Run

Month = 22
Staff size =   7.19
Code rate — 2334.11
Code remaining = 8808.14
Cumulative effort =   132.75
Investment =   154.30

Month = 23
Staff size =   7.32
Code rate = 2334.11
Code remaining =   244.80
Cumulative effort =   140.07
Investment =   163.93

At Project Completion:

Total time (months) =   23.03
Cumulative effort =   140.28
Investment =   166.60

Cocomo data for comparison:

Staff months = 393.61
Development time = 16.92
Cocomo type is **Embedded**

8.3 A Typical Analysis

A version of the program, given in the next section, written in C and run under the UNIX operating system on a Digital Equipment VAX 11/780 completed the example of the previous section in ~0.5 seconds of real time. Thus it is quite economical to use the model for parametric analyses of software development, as illustrated in the following table which shows the effect of varying the initial staff size on the total time, cumulative effort, and investment for a project whose other parameters are the same as the project analyzed in Section 7.3.

A Typical Analysis

Initial Staff	Total time (months)	Cumulative Effort	Investment (Staff Months)
3.0	31.12	122.69	153.72
5.0	23.03	140.20	166.60
7.0	18.95	155.68	177.29
9.0	17.50	183.44	208.82
11.0	16.67	210.78	237.19

As can be seen from the data in the table there is, not surprisingly, a trade-off between time and investment. The choice of the best initial staff size would then depend on other factors such as the expected revenues, the market window, the availability of staff, and the other projects that are in need of resources.

8.4 The Program

The following is a listing of the program whose output was presented above. The program is written in *Turbo Pascal*:

```
program model;
type Cocomo = (Organic,Semidetached,Embedded);
   criterion = (Optimal,FixedPercent,FixedTime,FixedStaff);
   PhaseType = (PreProduction,Production);
```

```
    projection = record
                     time, cost : real
                 end;
var staff_size,
    KDSI,
    interest_rate,
    coding_rate,
    loss_factor,
    a, b, c,
     {P(t + 1) = f(n) * [a + b * t + c * P(t)] + P(t)}
    t_staff, { staff time constant }
    productivity_gain,
    fraction_month,
    the_cost,
    the_time,
    Cocomo_mm,
    decisionParm,
    Cocomo_tdev:real;
    time:integer;
    Cocomo_type:Cocomo;
    decision_criterion:criterion;
    Cocomo_flag,criterion_flag:char;
    cumulative_effort,investment:real;
    IFilVar,OFilVar:Text;
    IFilName,OFilName:String[15];
```

186

The Program

```
   phase:PhaseType;

procedure FileSetup;
begin
   write('Enter input file name -> '); Readln(IFilName);
   Assign(IFilVar,IFilName); Reset(IFilVar);
   write('Enter output file name -> '); Readln(OFilName);
   Assign(OFilVar,OFilName); Rewrite(OFilVar);
end;

   { calculation of the communication loss factor }

function f(n:real):real;
begin
   f := n / (1 + loss_factor * ln(n))
end;

function new_p(p, n:real; t:integer):real;
begin
   new_p := f(n) * ( a + b * t + c * p ) + p
end;

function new_staff_size(staff_size:real):real;
begin
   new_staff_size := staff_size * exp(0.693147 / t_staff)
```

```
end;

    { project cost with no additional productivity work }

procedure program_cost(coding_rate,staff_size,KDSI:real;
                var month:projection);
var the_time, the_cost, fraction_month:real;
begin
    the_time := 0.0;
    the_cost := 0.0;
    while f(staff_size) * coding_rate <= KDSI do
    begin
        KDSI := KDSI - f(staff_size) * coding_rate;
        the_cost := the_cost * (1 + interest_rate / 1200) +
                    staff_size;
        the_time := the_time + 1.0;
        staff_size := new_staff_size(staff_size)
    end;
    fraction_month := KDSI / (f(staff_size) *
                        coding_rate * staff_size);
    the_cost := the_cost * (1 + interest_rate / 1200) +
                staff_size * fraction_month;
    the_time := the_time + fraction_month;
    month.time := the_time;
    month.cost := the_cost
```

The Program

```
end;

function power(a,b:real):real; { a to the power b }
begin
   power := exp(ln(a)*b)
end;


    { The calculation of the Cocomo model }

function mm(Cocomo_type:Cocomo):real;
var a,b:real;
begin
   case Cocomo_type of
      Organic: begin a := 2.4; b := 1.05 end;
      Semidetached: begin a := 3.0; b := 1.12 end;
      Embedded : begin a := 3.6; b := 1.20 end;
   end;
   mm := a * power(KDSI,b)
end;

function tdev(Cocomo_type:Cocomo):real;
var a,b:real;
begin
   case Cocomo_type of
      Organic: begin a := 2.5; b := 0.38 end;
```

```
      Semidetached: begin a := 2.5; b := 0.35 end;
      Embedded : begin a := 2.5; b := 0.32 end;
   end;
   tdev := a * power(mm(Cocomo_type),b)
end;


procedure calculate_Cocomo;
begin
   Cocomo_mm := mm(Cocomo_type);
   Cocomo_tdev := tdev(Cocomo_type)
end;


function one_more_month:Boolean;
var current_cost, new_coding_rate,future_cost,
    marginal_revenue, marginal_cost: real;
    this_month, next_month: projection;
begin
   program_cost(coding_rate,staff_size,KDSI,this_month);
   new_coding_rate := new_p(coding_rate,staff_size,time);
   program_cost(new_coding_rate,new_staff_size(staff_size),
            KDSI,next_month);
   current_cost := this_month.cost;
   future_cost := next_month.cost *
            (1 + interest_rate / 1200);
   marginal_revenue := current_cost - future_cost;
```

```
   marginal_cost := staff_size;
   case decision_criterion of
   Optimal:
   if (marginal_cost <= marginal_revenue)
               then one_more_month := TRUE
               else one_more_month := FALSE;
   FixedPercent:
   if (cumulative_effort <= decisionParm * Cocomo_mm)
               then one_more_month := TRUE
               else one_more_month := FALSE;
   FixedTime:
   if (time + this_month.time <= decisionParm)
               then one_more_month := TRUE
               else one_more_month := FALSE;
   FixedStaff:
   if (cumulative_effort + this_month.cost <= decisionParm)
               then one_more_month := TRUE
               else one_more_month := FALSE;
   end
end;

procedure write_monthly_data;
begin
   writeln('Month = ', time:3);
   writeln(OFilVar);
```

```
   writeln(OFilVar, 'Month = ', time:2);
   writeln(OFilVar, 'Staff size = ', staff_size:6:2);
   writeln(OFilVar, 'Code rate = ',coding_rate * 1000:7:2);
   if (phase = Production) then
      writeln(OFilVar, 'Code remaining = ',
              KDSI * 1000:7:2);
   writeln(OFilVar, 'Cumulative effort = ',
              cumulative_effort:7:2);
   writeln(OFilVar, 'Investment = ', investment:7:2);
   writeln(OFilVar)
end;

procedure write_summary_data;
begin
   writeln(OFilVar);
   writeln(OFilVar, 'At Project Completion:');
   writeln(OFilVar);
   writeln(OFilVar, 'Total time (months) = ',
              the_time:7:2);
   writeln(OFilVar, 'Cumulative effort = ',
              cumulative_effort:7:2);
   writeln(OFilVar, 'Investment = ', investment:7:2);
end;

procedure write_Cocomo_data;
```

```
var s:String[15];
begin
   writeln(OFilVar);
   writeln(OFilVar, 'Cocomo data for comparison:');
   writeln(OFilVar);
   writeln(OFilVar, 'Staff Months = ', Cocomo_mm:7:2);
   writeln(OFilVar, 'Development Time = ',
           Cocomo_tdev:7:2);
   case Cocomo_type of
      Organic : s := 'Organic';
      Semidetached : s := 'Semidetached';
      Embedded : s := 'Embedded';
   end;
   writeln(OFilVar, 'Cocomo type is ', s);
end;

procedure run_model;
var next_month_output:real;
begin
   phase := PreProduction;
      while one_more_month do
      begin
         cumulative_effort := cumulative_effort +
                   staff_size;
         investment := investment *
```

```
        ( 1 + interest_rate/1200) +
            staff_size;
    write_monthly_data;
    staff_size := new_staff_size(staff_size);
    time := time + 1;
    coding_rate := new_p(coding_rate,staff_size,time);
  end;
phase := Production;
writeln(OFilVar);
writeln(OFilVar, 'Switch to Production Phase');
writeln(OFilVar);
next_month_output := f(staff_size) * coding_rate;
while next_month_output <= KDSI do
begin
  KDSI := KDSI - f(staff_size) * coding_rate;
  cumulative_effort := cumulative_effort + staff_size;
  investment := investment * ( 1 + interest_rate/1200)
        staff_size;
  write_monthly_data;
  staff_size := new_staff_size(staff_size);
  next_month_output := f(staff_size) * coding_rate;
  time := time + 1;
end;
fraction_month := KDSI / (f(staff_size) * coding_rate);
investment := investment * (1 + interest_rate / 1200) +
```

```
                staff_size * fraction_month;
   cumulative_effort := cumulative_effort +
            staff_size * fraction_month;
   the_time := time - 1  + fraction_month;
   write_summary_data;
end;

procedure read_parms;
begin
   readln(IFilVar, KDSI);
   readln(IFilVar, staff_size);
   readln(IFilVar, Cocomo_flag);
   case Cocomo_flag of
      'O','o' : Cocomo_type := Organic;
      'S','s' : Cocomo_type := Semidetached;
      'E','e' : Cocomo_type := Embedded
   end;
   readln(IFilVar, coding_rate);
   coding_rate := coding_rate / 1000; { normalization }
   readln(IFilVar, a,b,c);
   readln(IFilVar, t_staff);
   readln(IFilVar, loss_factor);
   readln(IFilVar, interest_rate);
   readln(IFilVar, criterion_flag);
   case criterion_flag of
```

```
      'O', 'o' : decision_criterion := Optimal;
      'P', 'p' : decision_criterion := FixedPercent;
      'T', 't' : decision_criterion := FixedTime;
      'S', 's' : decision_criterion := FixedStaff;
   end;
   if Decision_criterion <> Optimal then
            readln(IFilVar, decisionParm);
end;

procedure write_parms;
var s:string[15];
begin
   writeln(OFilVar);
   writeln(OFilVar,
        'A list of the input parameter values:');
   writeln(OFilVar);
   writeln(OFilVar, 'KDSI  = ', KDSI:7:2);
   writeln(OFilVar, 'initial staff = ', staff_size:7:2);
   case Cocomo_type of
      Organic : s := 'Organic';
      Semidetached : s := 'Semidetached';
      Embedded : s := 'Embedded';
   end;
   writeln(OFilVar, 'Cocomo type is ', s);
   writeln(OFilVar,
```

```
          'nominal rate = ',coding_rate * 1000:7:2);
   writeln(OFilVar, 'a = ', a:5:3, '; b = ', b:5:3,
             '; c = ', c:5:3);
   writeln(OFilVar, 'staff time constant = ',
             t_staff:7:2);
   writeln(OFilVar, 'communication loss factor = ',
                       loss_factor:7:2);
   writeln(OFilVar, 'annual interest rate = ',
                       interest_rate:6:2, ' %');
   case decision_criterion of
      Optimal : s := 'Optimal';
      FixedPercent : s := 'FixedPercent';
      FixedTime : s := 'FixedTime';
      FixedStaff : s := 'FixedStaff';
   end;
   if decision_criterion <> Optimal then
             writeln(OFilVar, 'The decision parameter is ',
             decisionParm:7:2);
   writeln(OFilVar, 'Decision Criterion is ', s);
   writeln(OFilVar);
   writeln(OFilVar, 'Productivity Enhancement Phase');
   writeln(OFilVar);
end;

begin
```

```
    FileSetup;
    read_parms;
    write_parms;
    calculate_Cocomo;
    time := 1;
    cumulative_effort := 0.0;
    investment := 0.0;
    run_model;
    write_Cocomo_data;
    flush(OFilVar);
end.
```

Chapter 9

Transfer Pricing

In this chapter, we apply economic principles to the case where several organizations may be cooperatively involved in producing a set of software products to meet the needs of a variety of projects.

199

Software development is a labor-intensive activity, requiring the efforts of large numbers of highly trained programmers and computer scientist. A typical medium size project may require 50,000 lines of source code which, using typical industry productivity figures, is produced at the rate of 200 lines of source code per staff month. Thus, this typical medium size project takes over 25 staff years to produce. Increasingly, managers and software developers are concerned with software productivity.

A significant part of the effort in software development is the construction of the so-called *software tools* which are needed to support the programming effort. Software tools are programs which, like the scaffolding of a construction or a factory production line, are used to produce the deliverable end products but are not *per se* products, although they may be sold to other software developers. Some of the more familiar software tools are text editors, compilers, operating systems, and spreadsheets. Other perhaps less well known tools are project management software and program test drivers.

In a large software development firm there are many different projects each of which must use a set of software tools. Each project has a set of requirements which can best be met by a customized tool designed to its own specification. When a project develops its own tool set to its specifications the tools are generally not usable by other projects because:

200

Transfer Pricing

- The tool may have built-in restrictions which the developing organization accepts, but which are not acceptable to other users. For example, the organization may be using only one type of interactive terminal and may not have accounted for the needs of other types of terminals.

- The developing organization generally does not document the program well since they know how to use it. The documentation that does exist will be in the form of notes generally written for the convenience of the people who wrote the programs. No tutorial or reference material will exist.

- The project which wrote the program has no incentive to maintain and adapt the program for the needs of other users. In fact, it is often the case that the original programmers have gone on to new tasks and are unavailable so that no one really is able to help *without a substantial expenditure of resources.*

On the other hand, it is possible that it is more economical for several projects to develop a set of tools which meets their joint needs. This common tool set is known as a *common environment.* If so, it is appropriate that funds be assigned for developing the common tools and that the budget they allocate for the common tool set can include the cost of:

1. defining a set of requirements and specifications which satisfy the needs of the projects.

2. providing a set of manuals to satisfy the needs of users and maintainers of these common tools.

3. establishing and maintaining a support organization that can respond to trouble reports about the common tools, making the appropriate repairs, and providing enhancements where new needs are identified.

The problems which we then face are:

1. What economies for the firm can be achieved by the joint development for several projects of a set of common tools?

2. Assuming that a set of common software tools is developed by one or more of the organizations sharing this common set of tools, what is the appropriate transfer pricing mechanism that will provide incentives to the participants in the separate projects to act in such a way as to maximize the profits of the firm?

9.1 On Estimating the Costs and Benefits of Common Tools

9.1.1 Cost/Benefit Analysis In order to get some estimate of the size of tools, fifteen commonly used tools were sized [1]. The average number of lines of code per tool is ~5,500 and the standard deviation is about the same, with a full screen editor having 24,000 lines of source code causing the large variance. Nine of these 15 tools have between 3,000 and 7,000 lines of source code. So, in what follows, we have chosen 5,000 as the typical number of lines of code per tool.

Based on my experience, an estimate of the time to take an existing tool and provide standard user documentation and tutorial material is 1.5 - 2.0 staff years. An estimate of the time to produce a new tool is an additional 2.0 staff years for developing the source code.

If I assume that the basic common environment contains 10 tools, and that half of these exist, then a cost of ~30 staff years is needed to develop a common tools environment.

---

[1] These data were obtained from the UNIX source code which is stored on-line in many systems.

Transfer Pricing

To estimate the saving from a common set of tools, I assume that the time required for a project to identify a tool for use is two staff months, and the time to learn an inadequately documented tool is one staff month. The time to learn a well-documented tool is one week. I assume further that the number of tools used by a project is a function of project size as follows:

Project Size	No. of Tools
5	2
10	4
20	6
50	10

Then using the previously stated assumptions, the per project saving based on project size is:

Common Tools

(1) Project Size	(2) Total Search Time	(3) Total Learn Time	(4) Total Cost	(5) Common Tool Cost	(6) Savings
5	4	10	14	2.5	11.5
10	8	20	28	5	23
20	12	40	52	10	42
50	20	100	120	25	95

Note:

Column (2) is the number of tools used by the project times the search time per tool.

Column (3) assumes that each tool user learns and uses an average of two tools.

Column (4) is the sum of columns (2) and (3).

Column (5) is the time to learn to use a well-documented common; column (3) divided by 4.

Now weight these numbers for the number of projects of each size [2]:

---

[2] The data for this table are based on data from my organization.

Project Size	Number of Projects	Savings per Project	Total Savings
5	3	11.5	34.5
10	2	23	46
20	8	42	336
50	10	95	950

The total estimated savings, assuming that a common set of tools was in place, is 1,336.5 staff months. On the other hand, the cost of developing this common set of tools is only ˜360 staff months -- a very significant savings.

9.1.2 On the Difficulty of Validating Productivity Gains

Let us assume that the model given above is representative. Typical savings for a one year project would be on the order of 10%. But with programmer productivity variance as high as 100% it is virtually unprovable.

Example: Consider a project using a staff of ten people for one year. In the given model, without a common tool environment, there would be 92 staff months of programming. (Here we have used the previously assumed tool data, allocating 28 staff months to finding and learning the tools needed.) At an average rate of 200 lines of code, one might expect 18,400 lines of code, but productivity might range from 100 loc/month to 300 loc/month yielding a range of 9,200 loc to 27,600 loc.

With a common environment, using the model, one would expect 115 staff months of programming for an expected value of 23,000 loc - rather than 18,400 - and a corresponding range of 11,500 loc to 34,500 loc.

Let us assume that, in fact, we have achieved 23,000 loc. Is this due to increased productivity? In fact, even with no gain in productivity we would expect to achieve something like 23,000 loc from a 92 staff month effort perhaps one out of every three projects because of the variability of programmer productivity. Therefore, we would not expect such a test to be convincing.

The conclusion is that even if all other factors can be controlled, *it will be almost impossible to prove that a common programming environment increases productivity.* Nevertheless, even though it is virtually impossible to substantiate the savings due to a common set of tools using a small statistical test, I believe that it helps productivity. This answers the first question - namely, what economies are available by developing a common software environment - but leaves as an open question the problem of how to prove it.

9.2 Transfer Payment

Consider the problem of determining the price that organizations using common software tools should pay for these tools.

9.2.1 Basics In this section I use two simple examples to illustrate the basic principle of transfer pricing. Assume a company consisting of two (2) divisions, A & B, where Division A manufactures a product that is used by Division B. Division B sells to the market.

The methods of determining a transfer price are relevant to our problem because they should enable us to determine what price an organization producing a software tool should charge to other organizations that use that tool.

9.2.1.1 Example 1 The simplest case of transfer pricing is where there are two divisions, A and B, where A's product is used in the manufacture of B's product. Assume that there is a competitive external market in which A would be a *price taker*, and further that A produces enough to satisfy B's need [3]. What is the appropriate price for A to charge B to maximize the company's profit?

---

[3] Prof. J. R. Clark has pointed out that the assumption of sufficient production to satisfy B's needs is not necessary for the conclusion being drawn.

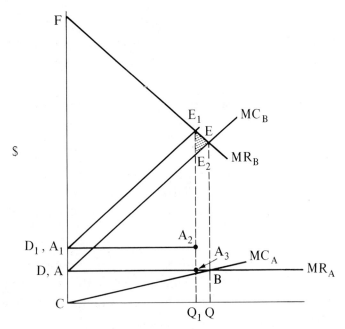

Figure 9.1 Transfer pricing - A charging too much

Figure 9.1 shows the *marginal cost* and *marginal revenue* curves of A and B. The *profit* is the integrated difference between marginal revenue and marginal cost:

$$\pi = \int_0^Q (MR - MC)dQ$$

Geometrically, this is the area between the marginal revenue and marginal cost curves. Thus A's profit is the area ABC and B's profit is the area DEF, and the firm's total profit is the sum of these areas.

Now suppose A charges a higher price than the market price. This shifts B's marginal cost curve to D_1E_1 so B now produces only Q_1. A's profit increases by $AA_1A_2A_3$. This is exactly the same as the profit decrease of B represented by the area $DD_1E_1E_2$ since $DD_1 = AA_1$. But B's profit is also decreased by the area EE_1E_2 and there is no offsetting gain for A [4].

Suppose, on the other hand, that A charges a lower price to B as shown in Figure 9.2. The analysis given above applies *mutatis mutandis* with net loss being represented by the area EE_1E_2 on Figure 9.2.

Further consideration shows that the assumption of a competitive market for A's product serves only to determine the price that A should charge B. But whenever there is an external market to determine A's price [5], a similar analysis would show that that is the price to charge B.

----

[4] A more careful examination would show that we have neglected a small triangular area which strengthens the argument.

[5] A's market need not be a competitive external market, so that A may not be a *price taker*.

Transfer Payment

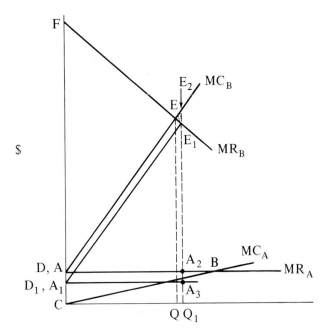

Figure 9.2 Transfer pricing - A charging too little

9.2.1.2 Example 2 Suppose that no external market exists; then the situation shown in Figure 9.3 prevails. The marginal cost curve is the sum of the separate marginal cost curves of the two divisions and the quantity to be produced can be determined from the composite marginal revenue - marginal cost curves. In that case the production level for A can be determined from Figure 9.3, since Q is the optimum quantity to be produced $(MR = MC)$ and the corresponding price for A should be the price which equals its

Transfer Pricing

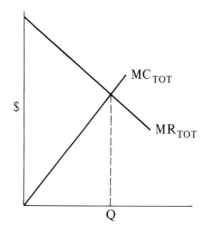

Figure 9.3 Transfer pricing - no external market

marginal cost at that quantity.

9.2.2 Application to the Common Software Problem

Let me summarize the principles which have been illustrated in the preceding section. If the transfer product is one for which an external market exists, then the price in that external market is the one that should be used as the transfer price. Based on that transfer price the firm can determine the optimal quantity to be produced. If there is no external market for the transfer product, then the total costs of the product including the cost of the transfer product should be used to determine the optimal quantity to be produced.

In the case where there is a price for the transfer product determined by the market, this solution is satisfactory because competitive factors will tend to drive prices down to eliminate economic profits, since those profits would encourage other producers to enter the market. However, in the case where no external market exists for the product, producers of the transfer product would have little incentive to produce the product efficiently, since their costs will be absorbed by the division which is marketing the final product.

In this case, factors like *X-inefficiency* can be significant in raising the price of the transfer product. X-inefficiency occurs when producers of the transfer product try to satisfy goals that do not necessarily maximize profits for the firm. Since the division producing the common software will have the charter of maximizing the use of common software they may use the following strategies:

1. Develop common software which attempts to meet everyone's requirements. Since cost is not a factor for the producer of the common software, the common software will be expensive and not especially efficient for any of the intended uses.

2. Push technology to make the software attractive from the point of view of computer science, though not necessarily economically attractive. This will result in a gain of prestige for the developers who will be able to pursue this strategy since they will not be cost-constrained.

In the absence of an external market for the product, it is not clear that an effective means can be devised for setting the requirements of common software or for establishing appropriate incentives that will encourage efficient development of that common software. A possible solution to these problems is to have the common software developed by a competitive bidding system within the firm. If several organizations have an expressed need for a particular software product, then each organization can establish a price they would be willing to pay for software that meets their specifications. A process of negotiation would ensue in which each would be free to bid to produce the software. This method would establish an internal market that would control prices and produce incentives, since once an organization had undertaken to develop a common software product at a specified price it would then try to be a profit maximizer.

If, as has been suggested earlier, there are significant savings to be made from the development of common software, then the prices offered by the organizations wishing to acquire that software would tend to provide excess economic profits for any organization that undertook to provide them. Other organizations sensing those economic profits would be encouraged to compete by bidding to produce the common software at a lower price, and the market mechanism would then tend to eliminate those economic profits.

9.2.2.1 Unresolved Issues

9.2.2.1.1 Selecting a Feature Mix In presenting the approach to developing a set of common software tools I have ignored the problem of determining the specifications of these tools. Here I shall consider this problem solely from the point of view of a producer wishing to decide on a set of features for a software product. In its simplest form the problem may be stated as follows:

We are given a set of features, $\{\, f_i \,\}$. This set of features is partially ordered so that for a given pair of features f_i and f_j with $i \neq j$ the features may either (1) be independent or (2) implementing f_i may require f_j. Assume further that for each subset, S, of the features there is an associated fixed cost, $C(S)$, where C may be assumed to be well-behaved in the sense that adding a feature increases the cost; i.e. $S \subseteq T$ implies that $C(S) \leq C(T)$.

We assume further that we know the demand function for each S, that is, the number of consumers who are willing to pay different prices for a product containing the subset of features S. Then for any particular feature set, S, we can maximize profits as usual. If, for example, marginal costs are negligible, as they may be in software production, and demand, $D(p)$, is a monotonic decreasing function of price, p, the revenue is $p*D(p)$ and we maximize revenue by setting the price at that value where the derivative of revenue with respect to price is equal to zero.

Now in principle we can solve the same problem for each subset S of the feature set. We would then obtain a profit maximizing solution for each S and could choose among these solutions.

If we neglect the marginal costs - since the cost of distribution may be as little as the cost for copying a tape or a floppy diskette - then the profit maximization of a software product containing a particular feature set depends primarily on the demand function for a product containing that feature set. For each demand function, the marginal cost approximates zero, so we can find the profit maximizing value and the corresponding maximum profit independent of marginal costs [6]. From the profit determined in this way we then subtract the cost and obtain a net profit for that feature set.

Example Suppose that we have a set of features, $\{a,\ b\}$, and possible products containing $\{a\}$, $\{b\}$, and $\{a,\ b\}$. Assume

---

[6] Martin Freeman has told me of a case where a well-known software vendor gave a seminar and distributed free to his audience non-reproducible diskettes of his latest software package. This suggest that although the retail price of the product was significant, the producer's marginal cost was negligible.

$$D(\{a\}) = 100 - p$$
$$D(\{b\}) = 150 - 2 * p$$
$$D(\{a, b\}) = 150 - 1.5 * p$$

One can check that for any p,
$$D(a,b) \geq D(a)$$
and
$$D(a,b) \geq D(b).$$

The revenue maximizing values are, assuming zero marginal costs,

$$p(\{a\}) = 50$$
$$p(\{b\}) = 37.5$$
$$p(\{a,b\}) = 50$$

The maximum revenues are 2500, 2813, and 3750, respectively. Assuming $C(\{a\}) = 1500$, $C(\{b\}) = 2000$, and $C(\{a,b\}) = 3000$, the best profit can be obtained by producing a product containing the feature a only.

9.2.2.1.2 Allocating the Costs Among the User Divisions We

have seen that in the case of a product for which there is an external market, divisions should pay the going market price. Where there is no external market, divisions using the product should pay the cost of the product. The question to be resolved is how to

Transfer Pricing

allocate the costs among the user divisions.

Again, assuming that the software production has negligible marginal costs, the optimal price for any product can be determined solely from the demand curve. Two possibilities suggest themselves:

1. A using division is charged a one-time fee for using the common software tool. (I include the possibility that no fee is charged.)

2. A division is charged on a per use basis.

Let us examine the second alternative of a fee which is related to the quantity sold. We shall do this by means of an example, but the conclusion appears to be more general.

Example. Consider a product with a demand function, $D = P - r*q$, and a unit price, **c**, for the common software tool use. Assuming that in software production there is negligible marginal cost, the use fee effectively shifts the demand function to

$$D = P - c - r*q$$

The optimal quantity 'sold' is now

$$q = \frac{P_0 - c}{2*r}$$

and the profit is $\frac{(P_0 - c)^2}{4*r}$.

However, the corporation also receives the additional profit from the use fee of

$$\frac{(P_0 - c)^* c}{2^* r}.$$

Combining these, we obtain as the total profit $k - \dfrac{c^2}{2^* r}$ which is maximized when $c = 0$.

9.3 Conclusion

We have applied some microeconomic principles to the study of a common software environment. Our tentative conclusions are:

1. A common software environment should reduce the cost of developing software by at least 5%.

2. It would be difficult to devise an experiment which could prove that such a savings results.

3. It is preferable for software tools to be produced so that they can be sold externally so that economic factors can motivate efficiency in their production.

4. Where an external market for software tools exists, internal users should pay the going rate.

5. Where no external market exists, a fixed fee, rather than a per use fee should be charged.

These are tentative conclusions which should be reevaluated in any case where the assumptions on which they are based do not apply.

Chapter 10

Summing Up

In this chapter I summarize the method of metaprogramming and review the economic model used to optimize the method. I review the rationale for the method and compare it to other approaches. Finally, I explain how economic models can be used to consider other resource allocation problems in computation.

The method of metaprogramming divides the software engineering cycle into two phases. In the first phase, a rapid prototype is constructed that validates the computational paradigms that are being used to construct the programs. Concurrently with the design of this computational architecture, a set of transformation tools is developed or customized to allow *efficient* production of the deliverable software. Following the initial phase, the system specifications are fixed in terms of the models that were prototyped, and the software is produced using the tools that were built during prototyping phase.

The methods of managerial economics are useful in formulating a dynamic model of the development process so that one can optimize the resource allocation between the two phases. The model presented in Chapters 7 and 8 is intentionally simplified so that one can see the concepts without added details that would obscure the main line of reasoning. In a more realistic setting, the model would be refined to account for the characteristics of the software being developed and the factors of production. It is also necessary to validate the growth model that characterizes the productivity gain curve, again subject to local variations. The development of these cost drivers and their inclusion into the model would make it more efficient, but, even without precise data, parametric studies can be very helpful in finding qualitative tradeoffs. Furthermore, there are always fairly large uncertainties and risk factors that must be accounted for, and even highly tuned software-costing models have a large variance [Mohanty].

In Chapter 2, I discussed quasi-expert systems. In fact, the method that is used to build many so-called expert systems resembles the method of metaprogramming. Typically, a first model is built using a relatively inefficient expert system shell. Then, after this prototype is validated, a set of tools is used to transform the prototype into a more efficient production version. There are, however, three elements of the method as presented here that are generally missing from such approaches. First, tool building often is deferred until the first model is completed and found to be too slow. The result is that the resources are not optimized; there would have been a gain if the tool building had started earlier and proceeded concurrently with the prototyping. Second, there is often little emphasis on formulating a clear model of the computational paradigm. Third, the production version is often produced with as much manual programming as the prototype.

The roles of the computational model and automation of the code generation are critical to the production of understandable code of high quality. An operational prototype or a functional specification can be validated, but the fact that they work does not mean that they are easily understood. Indeed, although interpreters can be considered as the first generation of operational prototypes and may help to speed up the production of programs, they do not

Summary

provide much to enhance the readability of the programs. Conversely, since interpreters allow you to more easily debug programs, they reduce the need for simple, well-structured programs.

The automation of the code generation is important, because it provides the best guarantee of uniformity in the product, and uniformity is an important component of quality. Further, software is generally modified and updated, and the degradation of code during its lifetime is well-known. Automating the code generation can be helpful, if the specifications can be kept clear and comprehensible through the use of a good computational model. In that case, revised specifications can be of as high a quality as the original specifications, and the software produced from those specifications will be as good as the original software release.

An approach to documentation that is promising is to use the primary program description as the source of the documentation. Examples of this approach are the natural language forms of expert system rules. Using a rather simple processor I have transformed the JMOS specifications, described in Chapter 3, into an English-like form. A more sophisticated program could produce a more polished natural language specification. Surely the quality of existing documentation warrants further research on the problems of producing up-to-date, accurate, and readable documentation.

10.1 Other Software Engineering Approaches

While the method of metaprogramming contrasts with the waterfall model of software development, it is intended as a disciplined approach with appropriate design and management controls. The prototype, the computational models, and the transformation tools should all be carefully controlled, using design reviews or walkthroughs. These inspections are important, because the method is designed to insure uniformity and ease of understanding. It could easily produce uniformly bad programs by the rule of GIGO (*garbage in - garbage out*). For example, a poor computational paradigm will inevitably lead to a poor program.

The method does not prefer any particular paradigm of computation. It should work equally well with a functional programming approach or with an object-based approach.

10.2 Other Applications of Economics to Software Engineering

In Chapter 10, I applied the methods of microeconomics to the software tool development within a firm where the question is how resources should be allocated among different entities within a firm. This is known as the *transfer pricing* problem. In order to present a model that could be understood, several simplifying assumptions were made, but as in the case of the software development model, it is possible to augment the model with additional elements. Here, I

224

Applications of Economics

briefly examine the economics of computation.

Suppose that we consider the costs of producing our software as consisting of two components: a cost of capital and a cost of labor, where we assume that to some extent the factors of production can substitute for each other. In terms of software engineering we might have a choice between hiring some additional staff or purchasing more computing resources. How do we make the choice? We can set up an equation, $P = P(K,L)$, where P is the total product, K is the cost of capital, and L is the cost of labor. If we maximize P, subject to the constraint that the sum of the costs of the factors remains constant, then the maximum total product is obtained when the marginal productivities per unit cost of capital and labor are equal. In other words, if by spending a fixed amount of money on staff we can increase production more than we could by spending the same amount of money on added computing resources, then that will produce the most product.

We may assume that the marginal productivity per unit cost for the firm as a whole can be determined, and is equal to the marginal productivity per unit cost of labor. The analysis of the tradeoffs between factors of production and the dynamics of such a model has been analyzed in managerial economics [Truett]. As in the economic models of Chapters 7-9, it is difficult to obtain quantitative data. However, the theory and models can be used in parametric and comparative studies.

10.3 The Role of Software Economics

Software engineering as a discipline to improve the productivity of programmers and the quality of software needs a well-developed body of economic theory and data. The economics of software engineering should provide guidance on the tradeoffs of resource allocation in software development.

Software economics is a new subject, and most questions about it do not have ready answers. With this book I have tried to contribute to the understanding and the development of software economics and software engineering.

Bibliography

ACM   *The Communications of the ACM*, September 1983.

Aho   Aho, A.V. and J.D. Ullman *Principles of Compiler Design* Addison-Wesley, 1977.

Alagic   Alagić, S. and M.A. Arbib *The Design of Well-Structured and Correct Programs* Springer-Verlag, 1978.

Allen   Allen, R.G.D. *Mathematical Economics*, MacMillan, 1959, 2nd Edition.

Banner   Banner, M.A. "A Survey and Critical Review of Expert Systems Research", in *Introductory Readings in Expert Systems.*

Basili   Basili, V.R. and Turner, A.J. "Iterative Enhancement: A Practical Technique for Software Development" in *Structured Programming Tutorial*, IEEE Catalog No. 75CH1049-6, Revised 1977.

Bassett   Bassett, P. "Software manufacturing Techniques and maintenance", Proceedings, NCC 1984, p. 357-365.

Beckmann   *Advanced Course on Software Engineering*,
                    ed. M. Beckmann, G. Goos, and H.P. Kunzi,
                    Springer-Verlag, 1973.

Beizer   Beizer, B. *Software Testing Techniques*, Van
                    Nostrand Reinhold, 1983.

Bennett   Bennett, J.L. *Building Decision Support
                    Systems*, Addison-Wesley, 1983.

Bergland   Bergland, G.D. and Gordon, R.D. *Tutorial:
                    Software Design Strategies*, IEEE Computing
                    Society, 1979.

Boehm 1981   Boehm,   B.W.   "Improving   Software
                    Productivity", CH1702, IEEE, 1981.

Boehm 1973   Boehm, B.W. "Software and its Impact: A
                    Quantitative Assessment", *Datamation*, May
                    1973, p.48-59.

Boehm 1976   Boehm, B.W. "Software Engineering" *IEEEE
                    Transactions   on   Software   Engineering*,
                    December 1976.

Brooks   Brooks, F.P. Jr. *The Mythical Man-month -
                    Essays on Software Engineering*, Addison-
                    Wesley, 1978.

Broome   Broome, P. and L.S. Levy "Primary Program
                    Descriptions: Why We Need a New Approach

Bibliography

to Correctness", *Proceedings of the 1978 Army Numerical Analysis and Computers Conference.*

Buckle   Buckle, .K. *Managing Software Projects*, American Elsevier, 1977.

Carberry   Carberry, S., H. Khalil, J.F. Leathrum, and L.S. Levy *Foundations of Computer Science*, Computer Science Press, 1979.

Cardenas   Cardenas, A. F. "Technology for Automatic Generation of Application Programs - A Pragmatic View", *MIS Quarterly*, September 1977.

Carlson   Carlson, E. D. " An Approach for Designing Decision-Support Systems" in *Building Decision Support Systems*, p.15-39.

Codd   Codd, E.F. "Relational Database: A Practical Foundation for Productivity", *Communications of the ACM*, February 1982, p. 109-118.

Cohen   Cohen, W.A. *Principles of Technical Management*, AMACOM, 1980.

Corbato   Corbato, F.J. and C.T.Linger in *Research Directions in Software Technology*, ed. P.

Bibliography

Wegner, MIT Press, 1978.

Davis

Davis,R. and Lenat, D.B. *Knowledge-Based Systems in Artificial Intelligence*, McGraw-Hill, 1982.

DeRemer

DeRemer, F. and Kron, H. "Programming-in-the-large vs Programming-in-the-small" *IEEE Transactions on Software Engineering*, June 1976, p. 80-86.

Dijkstra

Dijkstra, E.W. *A Discipline of Programming*, Prentice Hall, 1976.

Donelon

Donelon, W. S. "Project Planning and Control", *Datamation*, June 1976. Reprinted in *Tutorial: Management of Software*.

Ehrenreich

Ehrenreich, S.L. and W.A. Harris "JMOS: Stepping Outside with New Cost Control", *Bell Laboratories Record*, July 1985.

Ershov

Ershov, A.P. "Integrated Approach to Current Programs of Software Development", *Kibernetika*, No. 3, pp. 11-21, May-June 1984.

Ewers

Ewers, J. and Vessey, I. "The Systems Development Dilemma - A Programming Perspective", *MIS Quarterly*, June 1981, p.382-394.

Bibliography

Fairley   Fairley, R.E. *Software Engineering Concepts*, McGraw Hill, 1985.

Frank   Frank, W.L. *Critical Issues in Software - A Guide to Software Economics, Strategy, and Profitability*, John Wiley, 1983.

Freeman 1978   Freeman, M., Jacobs, W., and Levy, L.S. "On the Construction of Interactive Systems", *Proceedings NCC 1978*, p. 555-562.

Freeman 1976a   Freeman, P. and Wasserman, A.I. *Software Design Techniques Tutorial*, IEEE Computing Society, 1976.

Freeman 1976b   Freeman, P. "Software Reliability & Design: A Survey" *Proceedings 13th Annual Design Automation Conference*, IEEE 1976.

Friedman   Friedman, Lee S. *Microeconomic Policy Analysis*, McGraw Hill 1984, Chapters 8 and 15.

Gevarter   Gevarter, Wm. B. "An Overview of Expert Systems", NBSIR 82-2505, National Bureau of Standards, May 1982.

Goguen   Goguen, J., J. Thatcher, E.G. Wagner, and J.B. Wright "Initial Algebra Semantics", *Journal of the ACM*, January 1977.

231

Griswold

Griswold, R.E. *The Macro Implementation of SNOBOL4: A Case Study of Machine-Independent Software Development*, p.240, W.H.Freeman & Co, 1972.

Gwartney

Gwartney, James D., Richard Stroup, and J. R. Clark *Essentials of Economics*, Academic Press, 1982.

Gyllstrom

Gyllstrom, H.C., R.C.Knippel, R.C.Ragland, and K.E.Spachmann "The Universal Compiling System", *SIGPLAN Notices*, Dec. 1979, p. 64-70.

Hersey

Hersey, J. "Additional Views on Computer Soware", *Addendum to the CONTU Report*, 1976

Hirshleifer

Hirshleifer, Jack "On the Economics of Transfer Pricing", Journal of Business 29, (July 1956), p. 172-184.

IBM

IBM Systems Journal, Volume 19, No. 4, 1980 - Software Development.

Infotech

"The Use of Generators and Similar Techniques in the UK", *Infotech State of the Art Report on Programming Technology*, 1982.

Bibliography

Jackson

Jackson, M.A. "Information Systems: Modeling, Sequencing, and Transformations" *3rd International Conference on Software Engineering*, p. 72-81, 1978.

Jayachandra

Jayachandra, Y. "Telephony Software -- To Build or Padlock?" *Telephony*, Oct. 1977, p. 44-46.

Jensen

Jensen, R.W., and Tonies, C.C. *Software Engineering*, Prentice-Hall, 1979.

Jones 1979

Jones, C. "The Limits of programmer Productivity", *Proceedings Application Development Symposium*, SHARE, Inc., 1979.

Jones 1980

Jones, C. *Programming Productivity: Issues for the Eighties*, IEEE Computing Society, 1980.

Joshi 1980

Joshi, A.K., L.S. Levy, and K. Yueh "Local Constraints in Programming Languages -- Part I: Syntax", *Theoretical Computer Science*, 1980.

Joshi 1982

Joshi, A.K. and L.S. Levy "Phrase Structure Trees Bear More Fruit than You Would Have Thought", *American Journal of Computational Linguistics*, Vol. 8, No. 1, January 1982.

233

Bibliography

Keen

Keen, P. G. W. and Gambino, T. J. "Building a Decision Support System: The Mythical Man-Month Revisited" p. 132-172 in *Building Decision Support Systems* ed. J.L. Bennett, Addison-Wesley 1983.

Kernighan

Kernighan, B.W., and Plauger, P.J. *Software Tools*, Addison-Wesley, 1976.

Kidder

Kidder, T. *The Soul of a New Machine*, Little-Brown, 1981.

Kinnucan

Kinnucan, P. "Computers That Think Like Experts", *High Technology*, January 1984, p. 30-42.

Knuth

Knuth, D.E. *Fundamental Algorithms*, Addison Wesley, 1969, p. 178.

Lakatos

Lakatos, Imre *Proofs and Refutations: The Logic of Mathematical Discovery*, Cambridge U. Press, 1976.

Levinson

Levinson, E., Levy, L.S., and Salisbury, J.B. "CARL - Experience of an Application Using Clusters", *Proceedings NCC*, 1980.

Levy 1977

Levy, L.S. and R. Melville "The Algebraic Anatomy of Programs", *The Computer Journal*, Vol. 20, No. 4, 197.

Bibliography

Levy 1979   Levy, L.S. and A.K. Joshi "Alternatives to
                     BNF which preserve Syntactic Structure:
                     Syntax and Semantics - approaches and
                     problems", *Proceedings, CISS, Johns Hopkins*,
                     Spring 1979.

Levy 1980a   Levy, L.S. "The Cartesian Programmer and
                     the Hacker: Perspectives on Programming",
                     MicroDelcon 1980.

Levy 1980b   Levy, L.S. "Perspectives on Programming:
                     Applications to a First Graduate Course",
                     Proceedings MicroDelcon '80, p. 18-21.

Levy 1980c   Levy, L.S. *Discrete Structures of Computer
                     Science*, John Wiley & Sons, New York, 1980.

Levy 1981   Levy, L.S. and Freeman, M. "Simplicity is the
                     Key to Intellectual Control", MicroDelcon,
                     1981.

Levy 1982   Levy, L.S. "On Ultra-High Programmer
                     Productivity", *Micro-Delcon*, 1982.

Levy 1985   Levy, L.S. and Stump, H.T. "Inverted
                     Decision Tables and their Application:
                     Automating the Translation of Specifications
                     to Programs", *Bell Laboratories Technical
                     Journal*, February 1985.

Bibliography

Levy 1983	Levy, L.S. "A Walk through AWK", *SIGPLAN Notices*, December 1983.
Levy 1986	Levy, L.S. "A Metaprogramming Method and its Economic Justification", *Transactions on Software Engineering*, February 1986.
Linger	Linger, R.C. "Human Productivity in Software Development", CH1702, IEEE 1981.
Link	Link, A.N. "The Impact of Federal Research and Development Spending on Productivity", *IEEE Transactions on Engineering Management*, Vol. EM-29, No. 4, November 1982, p. 166 - 169.
Liskov	Liskov, B "A Design Methodology for Reliable Software Systems", in *Software Design Techniques Tutorial*, IEEE, 1976.
Liskov 1977	Liskov, B. A. Snyder, R. Atkinson, and C. Chafert "Abstraction Mechanisms in CLU", *Communications of the ACM*, August 1977, p. 564-576.
Marcotty	Marcotty, M., H.F. Ledgard, and G.V. Bochmann "A Sampler of Formal Definitions", *Computing Surveys*, Vol. 8, No. 2, p. 191-276.

Bibliography

Michie   *Introductory Readings in Expert Systems*, ed. D. Michie, Gordon & Breach Science Publishers, 1982.

Miller   Miller, E. and Howden, W.E. *Tutorial: Software Testing & Validation Techniques*, IEEE Computing Society, 1978.

Mohanty   Mohanty, S.N. "Software Cost Estimation: Present and Future" *Software-Practice and Experience*, Vol. 11. p. 103-121, 1981.

Niblett   Niblett, B. "Legal Aspects" in *Software Portability: An Advanced Course*, P.J. Brown, ed., Cambridge U. Press, 1977.

Nimtz   Nimtz, R.O. "Development of the Law of Computer Software Protection", *Journal of the Patent Office Society*, Jan. 1979, p. 3-43.

Pappas   Pappas, James L. and Eugene F. Brigham *Managerial Economics*, The Dryden Press, 1979, Chapter 11.

Parnas   Parnas, D.L. "Designing Software for Ease of Extension and Contraction" *3rd International Conference on Software Engineering*, p. 264-277, 1978.

Bibliography

Parr   Parr, F.N. "An Alternative to the Rayleigh
                        Curve Model for Software Development" *IEEE
                        Transactions on Software Engineering*, May
                        1980, p. 291-296.

Polya   Polya, G. *How to Solve It*, Doubleday Anchor
                        Books, 1957.

Putnam   Putnam, L.H. "A General Empirical Solution
                        to the Macro Software Sizing and Estimating
                        Problem", IEEE Transactions on Software
                        Engineering, July 1978, p.141-157.

Quinlan   Quinlan, J.R. "Fundamentals of the
                        Knowledge Engineering problem" in [Michie].

Ramamoorthy 1978a   Ramamoorthy, C.V. and So. H.H. "Software
                        Requirements & Specifications: Status and
                        Perspectives" *Engineering Research Lab
                        Report* UCB, June 1978.

Ramamoorthy 1978b   Ramamoorthy, C.V. and Yeh, R.T. *Tutorial:
                        Software Methodology*, IEEE Computing
                        Society, 1978.

Reddien   Reddien, C.R. "Legal Aspects of Software
                        Development" in *Software Engineering*, R.W.
                        Jensen and C.C.Tonies, Prentice Hall, 1979, p.
                        481-551.

Bibliography

Reifer   Reifer, D.J. *Tutorial: Software Management*, IEEE Computing Society, 1978.

Reynolds   Reynolds, J. *Cosers Report on Semantics of Programming Languages*, 1977.

Rice   Rice, J.G. "Build Program Techniques", *Infotech State of the Art Report*, 1981.

Rich   Rich, M. *Artificial Intelligence*, McGraw-Hill, 1983.

Rullo   *Advances in Computer Programming Management, Vol 1*, ed. T.A. Rullo, Heyden, 1980.

Runes   Runes, D.D., ed. *The Dictionary of Philosophy*, Philosophical Library, 1942.

Samuelson   Samuelson, P.A. and W.D. Nordhaus *Economics*, McGraw-Hill, 1985.

SE 1976   *Proceedings 2nd International Conference on Software Engineering*, October 1976.

SE 1978   *Proceedings 3rd International Conference on Software Engineering*, May 1978.

SE 1979   *Proceedings 4th International Conference on Software Engineering*, September 1979.

239

Bibliography

Shooman   Shooman, M.L. *Software Engineering: Design, Reliability, and Management*, McGraw-Hill, 1983.

SP   *Structured Programming Tutorial*, IEEE Computing Society, Compcon, 1975.

Stanley   Stanley, M. "Software Cost Estimating" *Royal Signals and Radar Establishment, Memorandum 3472.*

Tennent   Tennent, R.O. "Denotational Semantics of Programming Languages", *Communications of the ACM*, Aug. 1976, p. 437-453.

Thibodeau   Thibodeau, R. "An Evaluation of Software Cost Estimating Models" RADC-TR-81-144, Final Technical Report, June 1981.

Truett   Truett Lila J. and Dale B. Truett *Managerial Economics*, South-Western Publishing Co., 1980.

UNIX   *Unix System User's Manual*, Bell Laboratories, Inc.

Waltz   Waltz, D. L. "The state of the Art in Natural Language Understanding", Working Paper #27, U. of Illinois, Advanced Automation Group, Urbana, IL, 28 January, 1981.

Bibliography

Wasserman   Wasserman, A.I. & Gutz, S. *Communications of the ACM*, March 1982, p. 196-207.

Wegner   Wegner, P. "Vienna Definition Language", *Computing Surveys*, Vol. 4, No. 1.

Wichmann   Wichmann, B.A. "ADA is green", *Computer Bulletin*, Sept. 1979, p. 17.

Wilson   *The Essential Descartes*, ed: Margaret D. Wilson, Mentor Books, 1969.

Wolberg   Wolberg, J.R. *Conversion of Computer Software*, Prentice-Hall, 1983.

Yeh   *Current Trends in Programming Methodology - Vol. II : Program Validation*, R.T. Yeh, editor, Prentice-Hall, 1977.

Zave   Zave, P. "The Operational versus the Conventional Approach to Software Development", *Communications of the ACM*, Feb. 1984, p. 104-118.

Author Index

Subject Index

Ada, 70
Algol, 68, 108
APL, 75
application generators, 94n
application-code generator, 48
artificial intelligence, 28, 93n
AWK, 104–132
  built-in constructs in, 120–121
  data validator, 123–132
  pattern expressions in, 105, 115–120
  program parts, 106–107
  regular expression patterns in, 115–116
  relational operators in, 118–119
  rules and commands in, 108–113
  structure, 106–109
  symbols in, 116–117
  syntax, 113–115

Backus Naur Form, *see* BNF
backward chaining, 32
binding time, 95
blackboard model, 32
BNF (Backus Naur Form), 70–71, 113, 115
Bolzano, Bernard, 29n
Brook's Law, 87
Brook's Rule, 48, 82, 93

C (language), 105, 108, 121
call by reference, 72
CARL, 48, 49, 51, 54
  description, 45
Cartesian programmer, *see* software engineering, approaches
COCOMO model, 58n, 170; *see also* model software development, sample run; model software development, program
code generator, 46, 46n, 51, 54, 159, 222, 223; *see also* application-code generator

cognitive science, 28
common tools, 201–202
  cost/benefit, 203–206
  and productivity gains, 206–207
  and transfer payment, 208–219
competence-performance dilemma, 15
Computer Automated Route Layout, *see* CARL; metaprogramming
CONTU, *see* National Commission on New Technological Uses of Copyrighted Works (CONTU)
copyright, *see* software, legal status

data independence, 95
data validator, 121–132
decision table processors, 51–52
decision table, *see* inverted decision table
deep structure, 16
Dendral (system), 30
Descartes, Rene, 29n, 66
design methodology, *see* methodology
Digital Equipment VAX 11/780, 184
Dijkstra's weakest precondition, 72
documentation, 24–25, 54, 201
  approach to, 223
  and methodology, 93–94
  and semiotics, 69–70

empiricism, 67
empiricist, *see* software engineering, approaches
Euclid, 29n
Euclidean algorithm, 107, 109–111
expert system shell, 222
expert systems, 28–34, 95, 122
  characteristics of, 33–34
  definition, 28
  features, 29–30
  rules in, 32n
  versus quasi expert systems, 35–36;
    see also quasi expert systems

245